BECOMING YOUR OWN BEST FRIEND

NAMI LINDQUIST

SELF-STARTERS' STRATEGIES FOR SUCCESS SERIES

BECOMING YOUR OWN BEST FRIEND

HOW TO BUILD A BETTER RELATIONSHIP WITH YOURSELF AND CREATE YOUR OWN SUCCESS STORY

Published by Advantage, Charleston, South Carolina.
Member of Advantage Media Group.

ADVANTAGE is a registered trademark, and the Advantage colophon is a trademark of Advantage Media Group, Inc.

Printed in the United States of America.

10 9 8 7 6 5 4 3 2 1

ISBN: 978-1-64225-187-6
LCCN: 2020918561

Cover design by David Taylor.
Layout design by Carly Blake.

To younger Nami. I am stronger now because of you.

To Mama. You believed in me when I didn't.
Your unwavering sense of self made me into who I am today.

To Dad. You pushed me to see my potential and
stretched my vision of what I can become.

To my brother, Takuma. The only idiotic boy
I will keep by my side.

To my dog, Kuma. Good boy. Treat?

To all my readers who need this book. Enjoy.

CONTENTS

A Small Spark

I wanna see you be brave.

—SARA BAREILLES

I used to spend most of my days being afraid.

I used to worry about what other people thought of me.

I wasted so much time feeling small and powerless, unable to stand up for myself.

Some of you may know what that feels like. Maybe you're in a challenging space where backstabbing or jealous people are creating a toxic environment. Or maybe difficult relationships at home or at school have resulted in your feeling depleted, discouraged, and depressed.

For me, it was school. I was teased and bullied, especially by one girl who targeted me simply because I was best friends with her crush. I was quite shy and never had a big presence, so I was easy to pick on. I remember feeling so small and vulnerable, unable to stand up for myself. This girl spread rumors about me until, one by one, my friends drifted away, afraid to stand up for me because they didn't want to become her next target. Every day was a struggle. I received text messages threatening a "bad day," saying that she would "destroy my life" or "turn all of my friends against me" or suggesting that I would "regret everything" I supposedly had done.

I remember my body literally shivering with fear each morning when my mom would drive me to school and we would reach the school entrance. My parents tried to be supportive. In the mornings when my mom dropped me off, she encouraged me to breathe and shook my shoulders in an attempt to shake some of her courage into me. Every day, she wished me luck and said, "You've got this. You're going to stand up for yourself. You're going to prove to yourself that you can really be there—for you."

I spent a lot of time dreaming about being someone stronger and braver without truly understanding how to make that transformation. I would blast songs like "Brave," by Sara Bareilles, and wish that I had the ability she talks about in that song to really speak out my truth and be able to just let all of the pent-up negativity and frustrations inside of me cascade out.

But every day, I walked into that school, my hands clammy, fumbling with the ends of my sleeves, my head low, and my teeth nibbling my lip. I believed that nobody was on my side, that nobody wanted to associate with me, and that there was nothing I could do to change that.

Looking back, I'm not sure what I was really afraid of, but I faced a daily barrier, built from discomfort and from not knowing how to stand up for myself.

Above all, I was tired—tired of letting other people have that much control over me, tired of feeling anxious and fearful, tired of anger and regret. I wanted to be able to face myself in the mirror, knowing that I was willing to do whatever it took to defend that person looking back at me. I wanted to be proud of myself and what I stood for.

I WANTED TO BE ABLE TO FACE MYSELF IN THE MIRROR, KNOWING THAT I WAS WILLING TO DO WHATEVER IT TOOK TO DEFEND THAT PERSON LOOKING BACK AT ME.

I was desperate for an instant and lasting solution—maybe you are too—but the journey from powerless to powerful doesn't happen overnight. It takes hard work and a willingness to accept setbacks without letting them become roadblocks. What I needed most was someone who understood, who could share tips and strategies to help me feel confident and brave. A friend.

If this is your story, too, I have good news. It does get better—I can be that friend for you. And I can help you learn how to become your own best friend. Your change can start right now, today. There are steps you can take to boost your self-confidence and encourage and empower yourself. There are techniques you can use to adjust your mindset, attitudes, and behaviors in ways that are positive and healthy.

I have been where you are, desperate for tools and strategies to help me improve my sense of worth, to equip me to shift my focus away from other people and concentrate on my own plans and dreams. I've combed through resources, read books and blogs, listened to podcasts, all in an effort to collect as much wisdom on this topic as possible. I've learned how to demand respect—not just from others, but also from myself. I've discovered the power of challenging myself by facing things that scare me and using that fear as an opportunity, rather than a barrier.

I'm giving you the guidebook I needed, written by someone who has navigated the steps from powerless to powerful. It's full of practical advice, with exercises you can follow to increase your confidence and inspiration to keep you motivated and focused on achieving your goals.

I've written this book at the age of seventeen, and while I'll be sharing my experiences, I'll also include the perspectives of other self-starters and data from science and psychology. No matter your age, I want to encourage you. No matter your story, I want to help you write a better next chapter.

I believe that self-confidence is the most powerful skill you can possess. Self-confidence equips you to master those crippling thoughts of anxiety and worry so that you can focus on completing tasks and achieving your goals.

Stop for a minute and consider the word I used there—self-confidence is a *skill*. It's not just a gift or a personality trait that some lucky people have from birth. You can learn how to develop confidence, practicing simple techniques as you gain assurance and using that confidence to face bigger and bigger fears.

But in order to find your confidence, you have to *begin*. Start wherever you are right now. I had to do something to change my situation, so with the encouragement of my parents, I got started. Those first steps were tentative. I role-played with my parents at night, crying while I practiced things to say to the girl who was bullying me. I repeated powerful responses over and over until they flowed naturally … right up until the moment when I would see that girl the next day, and I would freeze. I felt weak, miserable, hopeless. I didn't know what it felt like to stand up for myself, but I was desperate to learn.

That small spark—the desire to become confident and powerful—has grown over the years. I promised myself long ago that I would not let myself be defined by a bully or by my own fears. And slowly, by practicing the strategies I'll share in this book, a new Nami has taken shape. I'm bolder, more confident. I've gone through hell and emerged on the other side grateful for what I've experienced, because it's taught me to love myself so strongly that I'm my own best support system.

I'VE GONE THROUGH HELL AND EMERGED ON THE OTHER SIDE GRATEFUL FOR WHAT I'VE EXPERIENCED, BECAUSE IT'S TAUGHT ME TO LOVE MYSELF SO STRONGLY THAT I'M MY OWN BEST SUPPORT SYSTEM.

My desire to become more powerful began as a small spark, one that the bullies and the critics and my own fears and doubts threatened to extinguish at first. But I've learned how to harness that light, to nurture the flame and help it grow into a blaze so strong that it can't be put out.

I believe that you have that light inside you, just waiting for you to harness it. *Becoming Your Own Best Friend* is born from the belief that you can learn to lead a more effective, successful, and confident life. You may be at a hard moment in your journey, but you're not alone. This book is designed to be a guide, an encouragement, a source of support when you need it, and a push when you're slipping back into bad habits.

In the pages that follow, I'll share the tips and tricks that have helped me become a true self-starter, someone with initiative and the confidence to ignore those critical voices (including my own) that would hold me back from achieving my goals. We'll start by discussing strategies that will help you increase your comfort and build confidence. This is an opportunity to step back, do a deep dive into the roadblocks and obstacles you've set up for yourself, and identify how best to maximize your strengths and minimize your weaknesses.

We'll explore techniques to equip and empower yourself—to really begin to build strength. I'll share proven tips that have helped me shift my focus from outside sources of validation to a confident inner voice celebrating the person I am in this moment. You'll find opportunities to reflect on past successes and create healthy motivators to encourage you when you encounter setbacks.

Finally, we'll discuss strategies you can use to create your own plan for success. I'll share the steps that worked for me, exercises that helped me become more proactive and more creative at identifying opportunities—and seizing them. We'll consider some easy-to-apply responses to the failures and learning curves that are an inevitable part of trying something new, and end with a focus on goals that will help you implement these new techniques and equip you to become more confident and more effective.

This book is designed to be a resource that you can turn to again and again, so make it your own. Write notes in the pages; add comments and thoughts that occur to you as you read each section. Jot down your goals, and track your progress.

I've tried to make sure that it's easy to find what you need in each chapter, breaking important content into different sections. Here's how:

- **Drop In**: In these sections I'll share my own experiences and those of other self-starters who've encountered obstacles and learned how to transition from fearful to fearless.

- **Mull Over**: Here we'll focus on the specifics of each challenge and examine the skills you'll want to develop to face it.

- **Psych Out**: We'll turn to the experts for some data in this section, learning about the science and psychology behind mindset, confidence, self-esteem, and personal growth.

- **Power Up**: Each chapter ends with a section that contains practical exercises so that you can immediately begin to use the knowledge and tips in your own life.

My hope is that this book will be a guide to help you navigate challenging experiences. I want to share the secrets of the practical step-by-step process I've developed, one that has helped me build firm self-confidence and inspired the kind of growth I used to dream of and have now achieved. I encourage you to take these tips and make them your own, molding them into strategies that work for your circumstances and your personal goals.

It's funny—the girl whose bullying started me on this journey, the one who once left me feeling so powerless? Well, we still attend the same school; I see her in the hallways sometimes, but her existence doesn't matter to me anymore. The first time she saw me after summer break, she kept looking at me, and she seemed confused, as if I was a completely different person. That's because I am.

I'm more self-reliant, bolder, braver.

And now it's time for you to create your own success story.

NOTES

_____

_____

_____

_____

_____

_____

_____

_____

_____

_____

_____

_____

_____

_____

_____

_____

_____

_____

CHAPTER ONE

Get to Know Yourself

Knowing yourself is the beginning of all wisdom.
—ARISTOTLE

Y ou can't truly get to know yourself and define who you are if you identify yourself using the labels other people have created for you. It's sometimes tempting to let other people do the work for you, defining you based on how they see you. But when you take the time to carefully study what you love, how you've processed experiences, and the things you're passionate about, you'll have a much clearer picture of who you truly are and be better equipped to move forward confidently toward your goals. Knowing yourself and understanding how you function are crucial to feeling comfortable and confident. How can you be your own best friend if you don't know who that best friend truly is?

In this chapter, I'll share some strategies I've used to connect with who I really am and claim an identity that is honest and positive. I'll also discuss techniques that help me to reframe experiences so that they motivate me, rather than hold me back.

DROP IN

The crisp September air brushed against my face as I hurried out of my new high school to which I had just transferred.

Finally.

I popped my earbuds in and cranked up the music—usually rap, but sometimes hard-core rock. Anything loud enough, powerful enough, to drown out the noise from the other students around me and my own nagging thoughts.

As a transfer student at a high school infested with cliques, I experienced every day as a challenge. Every day, I struggled with feeling uncomfortable, feeling alone, and trying to find my place in a school that wasn't open to new people like me. Every day, I would make sure that I was being approachable and friendly, but I was never able to completely integrate into the preexisting cliques. It was almost like they were obligated to stay within their own friend group and not speak to new people.

The walks to and from school were awful. In the mornings, walking up the hill to school, I couldn't stop thinking about the people I would have to deal with, worrying that my feelings of awkwardness would spoil another day. Going back down the hill, I'd replay every interaction, wanting only to get back to my room, my escape zone, so I could cry.

I made new casual friends at school I would say hi to in the hallway and talk about schoolwork with, but these didn't develop into the deeper, more meaningful friendships that I was looking for. When I opened up about my struggles to someone I had met at that school, they said that I was a "nerd" and "socially awkward" and that was the reason why I was having such a tough time finding my people at the new school. I am typically very confident and know when people are just trying to be mean, so I'm not really sure why their words affected me. But in that environment, where every day already felt hard and awkward, those phrases somehow attached themselves to me, and I began to believe them. I began to accept the labels that were being stuck on me, and I started internalizing the opinions of other people.

For a few months, I would blast music on those walks, trying to prepare for the day, using the music to shield myself from the negativity around me—negativity that I internalized. As I walked up and down the hill, I would think, "Why am I so boring? Why am I so lame to talk to? I had friends at my previous school, so why couldn't I make friends here?"

Lunchtime at school was the worst, because you're set free. No assigned seats, no teacher directing interactions or distracting you with assignments. Just a huge, noisy cafeteria where everyone seemed to have friends to eat with. Everyone seemed happy; everyone belonged.

In that moment, I didn't want to be unique or different. I just wanted to fit in and find my place. I would always panic during lunch, trying to figure out how I would spend those thirty minutes and whom I would spend them with.

However, after a while, I started noticing that many people actually also spent lunchtime alone, whether that was driving by themselves to the local 7-Eleven or studying in the library for their upcoming tests. When I made this realization, my narrative of lunchtime started to change.

For the longest time, I had a script in my head of what high school lunch period should look like—me surrounded by friends, chatting happily. But what would happen, I began to wonder, if I rewrote that script, if I changed the setting so that a good lunch period meant that I was sitting in a peaceful place, maybe talking to someone in the library and doing homework or studying for a test? What if that became the framework for a successful lunch? As a competitive student, I felt that every minute of the day counted. So why not use lunch as my work period?

I realized that I could spend lunchtime worrying about where I should sit in the cafeteria and whom I could eat with, or I could spend it studying in the library. It was peaceful there; no one made fun of me for reading or doing homework. I could work on projects that brought me joy, like this book!

> **I SLOWLY STARTED TO UNDERSTAND THAT IN A SITUATION IN WHICH I FELT POWERLESS, I ACTUALLY DID HAVE SOME POWER. I COULD CHANGE HOW I WAS MEASURING SUCCESS.**

I slowly started to understand that in a situation in which I felt powerless, I actually did have some power. I could change how I was measuring success. I could change how I framed my experiences, using things I could control—using my own labels for what high school lunch period looked like for me. This epiphany felt like a huge weight had been lifted off my shoulders because this meant I didn't need to squeeze myself into a mold that would never perfectly fit.

It's a strategy that I then began to use in other ways. On the walks to and from school, I recorded voice memos, discussing my day as if I were talking to a friend.

Hey, I'm just walking home from school and wanted to chat. Today was pretty bad. I got to class late and …

When I had my earbuds in, no one could tell whom I was talking to. It was an opportunity to journal out loud, to sort through the stresses of the day and make sense of my experiences.

In that way, I was able to step back from my own feelings and assess them more neutrally, as I would for a friend. I could remind myself of my goals and priorities.

You have a job to do right now, as a student. You want to get into your top university. That's your goal for your future. The best schools only select a few students from a high school—they're looking for the students who are unique, who stand out. So you can ignore what other students are saying, the ways they're putting you down, because they're your competition. If they're telling you that you're odd or different, that proves that you're doing the right thing. That shows that you're accomplishing the goal of standing out.

I took those labels that came from someone else—"nerdy" and "different"—and transformed what they meant to me. I used to hate those labels, wanting to break free from those words that made me feel confined and inferior, but after reframing how I would receive these labels and what they meant to me, I learned how I could empower and motivate myself to keep chasing my ambitions.

Eventually, I found great friends at my new school. Though the first bit of the school year was rough, it was worth working through it because I learned a lot about myself and others.

MULL OVER

You are not stuck in the identity someone else has given you. If you dedicate some time to truly getting to know yourself—to doing some self-analysis—you'll be able to figure out which labels are true and honest and determine your identity for yourself.

Too often, the labels we use for ourselves can be judgmental. We aren't always comfortable praising ourselves or even doing an honest self-analysis. We tend to dig deep into our faults and criticize ourselves for not achieving a picture of who and what we believe is "perfect."

Though I do believe that we should own up to our shortcomings and address our areas of improvement, we shouldn't only focus on the negatives of ourselves. Why should we be kinder to other people than we are to ourselves? Why shouldn't we be our own best friends?

Self-analysis is something that most people initially feel uncomfortable doing because it's not something we talk about much in society. Sometimes, when people start their self-analysis, they tend to only look at the negatives of themselves or the situations on which they are focused and fall into a rabbit hole of self-doubt and counterproductive negativity. To avoid this, my advice is to be as neutral as possible. When you're reflecting on something you did, on the events of the day, on a challenging conversation, don't give in to the temptation to say, "That was terrible." Just focus on what you did and why you did it.

This ability to comfortably analyze yourself is a critical skill that will help you identify your motivators and determine what really matters to you. I use it as a way to redirect myself to things that are meaningful. I don't want to waste time and energy on BS, on people unworthy of my time, and on petty worries. I want to be busy with things that matter to me.

By taking that step to talk over the day with myself, it quickly becomes clear what actually is meaningful. I can prioritize my focus and direct my energy to the goals that deserve my time.

It's tempting to use other people or external things to make up for whatever may be lacking in your life. Don't do it. You'll waste time and energy finding other people, but not yourself. Do the hard work of examining whatever is going on inside you, reinforcing your goals and dreams, and reflecting and learning from each experience.

Though it is sometimes helpful to have someone analyze your issues for you to get a different perspective, it is just as important to be able to analyze yourself accurately.

DO THE HARD WORK OF EXAMINING WHATEVER IS GOING ON INSIDE YOU, REINFORCING YOUR GOALS AND DREAMS, AND REFLECTING AND LEARNING FROM EACH EXPERIENCE.

So what does this look like? How do you transition from self-criticism to self-analysis?

Let's use an example everyone can relate to: the conversation replay. At some point, you've probably had a conversation with someone that didn't go the way you wanted. Maybe it was a confrontation that you were prepared for, had rehearsed, and were ready to have, but your emotions took over, and you lost your focus. Maybe it was an unexpected argument that blew up before you even knew what had happened. Or maybe it was a conversation in which, as soon as the words were out of your mouth, you knew that you had said the wrong thing.

We've all had those conversations. If you're like me, you've probably then done the replay, going over and over what was said, how it was said, and what should have been said. And going through this cycle enough to drive yourself insane.

This is an example of where it's helpful to be as neutral as possible. Don't let your emotions and how you feel about your actions define your view of the actions you took. When analyzing a situation like the conversation replay, focus on the *why*. Why did you respond in the way you did? Why weren't you able to express your thoughts as clearly as you wanted to? It may have been because you suddenly became nervous, or because you didn't have a clear idea of how you wanted to express your thoughts before you started speaking.

As soon as I shift to that perspective—the perspective of a neutral observer—I can quickly identify the real source of the problem. Maybe my thoughts got cloudy because I was afraid or angry or frustrated. Maybe I wasn't prepared. Maybe I was prepared but didn't anticipate emotionally what it would feel like to be having that conversation.

Once you identify the answer to the "why," you can prepare a solution. If you weren't prepared, maybe you need to rehearse the next conversation so that you'll be able to respond more confidently. Maybe you hadn't realized that there was something important you needed to express; now that you know this, you can decide how and what you need to say. Maybe the emotions overwhelmed you; if that's the case, you may find it helpful to make a list of steps you can take to be better prepared for the emotions you may experience.

It's important to take that step back and understand why you responded the way you did, but it's not enough to simply say, "Oh, this is what happened." After identifying the reason behind your actions, you need to create a plan so that you can execute what you wanted initially. If you're going through a conversation replay, you may want to go back and have a follow-up conversation. If so, use the knowledge you gained from doing self-analysis to better position yourself for when you have that follow-up conversation. As my dad always repeats from Benjamin Franklin, "By failing to prepare, you are preparing to fail." If you fall short on maximizing the knowledge you gain from self-analysis for future application, you are preparing yourself for future dissatisfaction.

I know that it's hard to do that, to go back and try again. This is where you need to be careful about the labels you use. If you say, "I'm a failure" or "I get too nervous" or "I'm too emotional," you're preparing yourself to fail instead of succeed.

Don't fall into a shame spiral. Things will go wrong. It's OK. This is part of the process. Growth is not a linear action, and all the failures or unwanted outcomes teach us something new, as long as you are actively trying to learn from them. It's all about what you make of it and with what mindset you choose to accept outcomes. Trust the process, and trust yourself to be able to deliver and achieve what you're trying to do.

PSYCH OUT

The benefits of self-examination have been studied by scholars since Sigmund Freud first popularized the concept of self-analysis in the beginning of the twentieth century. Contemporary philosopher James Gould suggests that self-examination is a key to living a full, moral life.[1]

"A main cause of behavior is what we believe, not what happens to us," Gould says. In order to change behavior that seems automatic, he suggests that you must be more intentional, exercising your self-reflection muscles just like you would a physical muscle.

That pause, that step back, helps you gain the perspective and insight to make better choices. As Gould explains, "The purpose of self-examination is not to make us feel guilty about our failures, but is to enable us to identify and learn from our mistakes and to strengthen our resolve to change. Careful self-analysis is an important means of self-transformation."

---

1   James Gould, "Becoming good: The role of spiritual practice," *Philosophical Practice* 1, no. 3, 135–147 (2005).

There are several tests you can take to build understanding of yourself and the forces that motivate you. One is the DiSC Assessment (https://www.discprofile.com/), which helps you understand how you respond to conflict, how you solve problems, what causes you stress, and what motivates you. Through your responses to questions, you begin to identify your behaviors in four key areas:

- *Dominance*: Measures how results oriented you are, and how likely to accept challenges.

- *Influence*: Measures how much emphasis you place on relationships and collaborating with others.

- *Steadiness*: Reflects how cooperative and sincere you are.

- *Conscientiousness*: Measures how much emphasis you place on quality and accuracy.

Another helpful self-assessment test is the Myers-Briggs Type Indicator (https://www.mbtionline.com/). This test focuses on what makes you unique, generating understanding that you can use to foster a growth mindset. Myers-Briggs can help you identify which of sixteen personality types is most like you by measuring introversion or extroversion, sensing, intuition, thinking, feeling, judging, and perceiving.

I find these kinds of assessments very useful. There are several versions available online. They are a fun and interesting way to begin practicing the skill of self-assessment and equipping yourself to create a development plan to identify areas you may want to change.

For example, when I took the DiSC Assessment, I discovered that my Dominance score was 99 out of 100. That means I prioritize taking action and accepting challenges. I'm motivated by competition and success but struggle with being patient when things (or people) move slowly. Realizing this, I have been working on the idea of "trusting the process" and knowing that as long as I am doing what I need to be doing, there is no reason why things should go wrong. These reminders have helped me work better with others whose pace of work is not as quick as mine, and they have helped lower my levels of stress.

POWER UP

So let's talk about what this means for you. What steps can you take to reflect on your experiences in a neutral way, learn from your mistakes, and reframe your experiences so that you can define success in simple, achievable goals?

As a good first step for those who are not used to self-analysis, I recommend taking an online assessment. Learning more about your personality type will help you understand your behavior and set achievable goals. Though these tests are typically good at generalizing personalities, remember to take some results with a grain of salt and not get *too* caught up thinking that the test results exactly reflect your personality.

Another good step is journaling, either writing down your experiences or—as I like to do—talking through them using voice memos. Be factual, almost like a journalist, as you describe what happened and how it felt in that moment. Try to avoid labeling something in terms of being "good" or "bad," but simply record the experience, and make note of any emotions that accompanied it.

You may discover—as I often do—that if you do this kind of factual reporting, it makes it much easier to examine experiences in a neutral way and even come up with solutions before you've finished describing the event. I like to think of this state of neutrality as a detachment of my logical side from my emotions. I simply use my logical side to state what occurred in the moment, and I put my feelings about those occurrences aside as I analyze.

If it feels challenging to do this—if you're struggling because the event or the conversation or experience still sparks a lot of emotion—you may want to analyze it using a web diagram. Put the problem you're struggling with in the middle, and then add all of the explanations branching out from it. Think about why this problem exists—its reasons—and add those. Next, add more branches to represent how the problem is affecting you and any ways in which this problem is causing you stress. Now, assess those factors in terms of priority, identifying the ones you need to address first. The purpose of this kind of diagramming is to help you see the areas that need your immediate attention, the ones that you want to prioritize first to help solve this problem. By analyzing in this way, you can visualize your thoughts and have them in front of you so you don't feel overwhelmed trying to sort through them in your head. Being able to sort it out visually and write it down like in the following web diagram example helps me avoid the temptation to just keep thinking and worrying. Instead, that visual diagram gives me the ability to ask, "What are the factors contributing to this problem? Which ones are the most important, and which ones are the biggest?"

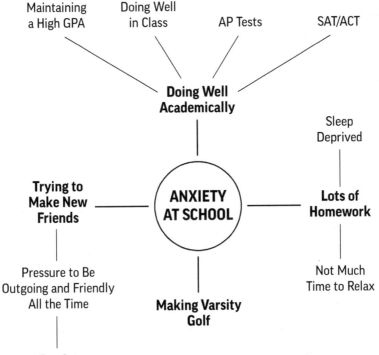

PRIORITY LIST

1) Lots of homework
- Watch less Netflix and study instead
- Stop using my phone as much and use that time to finish homework
- Try to get some homework done in class

2) Doing well academically
- Ask teachers for help when I need it
- Get an SAT/ACT prep book and start studying

3) Making varsity golf
- Wake up one hour earlier in the morning to practice golf

After creating a web diagram, I'm able to make a priority list, so whenever I feel anxious about whatever challenge I am trying to overcome, I can look at my list and understand, "OK, this is the direction I chose to go in. Now, all I have to do is execute that plan." This list acts like my North Star. When my mind is distracted and I feel as if I have no clear direction that I am working toward in the moment, I look over the list, and my mind can then easily prioritize rather than being distracted by my small nagging thoughts.

I realize that it can feel uncomfortable and challenging to do this kind of self-analysis, to set aside emotions and criticism and simply look at yourself, your experiences, and your environment in a very neutral way. But when you build that habit, it becomes easier to define your environment instead of being defined by it. You can choose the labels you give yourself, and you can determine a plan of growth that is customized to your needs so you can maximize the time you spend working on yourself. Understand yourself well enough so you know what you need and what kinds of things work best for you. This way, you'll be able to be the most effective best friend you can be for yourself.

NOTES

_____

_____

_____

_____

_____

_____

_____

_____

_____

_____

_____

_____

_____

_____

_____

_____

_____

_____

_____

CHAPTER TWO

Hold Your Own Hand

*Courage is not the absence of fear but
the ability to act in spite of it.*
—FRANKLIN ROOSEVELT

I f you're someone who's terrified at the thought of public speaking, you're not alone. The idea of sharing your views and letting your voice be heard in front of a group of people can be very uncomfortable, and that discomfort gets magnified as the size of the group increases.

I've learned to find comfort in the midst of that discomfort and to use that fear as a motivator.

Here's my story.

DROP IN

I was that shy girl in the classroom who never volunteered, who never raised her hand. Why? Often, I was just too self-conscious, focusing on what other people might think of me.

That's the girl—the quiet girl in Japanese class—whom the teacher asked to lead an assembly celebrating the partnership between our school and a school in Kobe, Japan. An assembly in which three hundred students and teachers—from our school and the school in Kobe—would be sitting in chairs looking up at me on stage. An assembly in which I would have to speak Japanese, a language in which I was definitely not fluent.

I'm still not sure why she asked me. But I clearly remember my thoughts.

No. Absolutely not. I can't stand up there and speak confidently in front of two schools in English, let alone Japanese. It would be so embarrassing if I made a mistake. They would all make fun of me. I'd have nowhere to go. I'd be up on that stage, red faced, all alone.

That was one part of what I was thinking. But there was also another part, a very small voice, which was saying this:

It would be pretty cool to be the face of my Japanese class.

I've discovered that we have these moments all the time, the moments when fear and courage battle it out and you have to choose which voice you're going to listen to. It's up to you.

But at the time, I was still looking to other people to shape my choices. I knew that my face communicated my fear, my discomfort. I stared at the teacher, thinking that if I just waited long enough, she would decide for me by saying something like, "It seems like you don't want to do it. I'll ask someone else."

But she didn't. She just waited.

There were no excuses, no easy outs. Just that same quiet voice inside.

Nami, this is not something scary to run away from. This is an opportunity.

I took a deep breath and looked at the teacher and said, "Sensei, I'll do it."

I spent the next two weeks feeling the fears and doubts—but also preparing. I learned that I was going to serve as the MC for the assembly. I was responsible for speaking for about ten minutes, first when introducing the principal of our school and the principal of our partner school in Japan, and then talking about the benefits of our partnership and expressing thanks on behalf of our school for that relationship. Then, I was responsible for introducing the traditional Japanese song our class would be performing, discussing our preparation, and explaining why the song was meaningful to us. After each performance, I had to walk back onto the stage, thank the performers, and introduce the next song.

I wrote down everything that I was going to say and practiced saying those words out loud, over and over. I practiced at home, in the hallways at school, anywhere I could.

Then the day of the assembly came. There were no rehearsals, no opportunities to prepare ahead of time for the experience of standing up in front of all those people.

I'd love to tell you that I confidently walked out onto that stage, but that wouldn't be honest. I had to fight my fear before the assembly and every minute that it lasted. I was terrified, and I could hear my nerves in my shaky voice as I tried to speak the words I'd practiced. I felt my face getting red, but I kept going. I was determined to finish, and I did.

It's hard to describe the overwhelming, absolute relief I felt when it was over and I could walk off that stage. At first, it was a simple sensation of having survived, of no longer being embarrassed and nervous but just very glad that it had ended.

And then, something else took over.

Pride. Self-respect.

Those were not sensations I knew very well, so it was almost shocking to realize that the critical voice that so often prevented me from saying or doing things had been replaced by a different voice, with a different message:

I was the only person chosen to represent my school on that stage. I stepped outside my comfort zone. I said yes and pulled through.

I was so proud of myself and glad that I'd done it. I've learned to love that feeling of adrenaline when facing something that terrifies me, and the absolute relief and clear sense of accomplishment when it's over. It's that "no pain, no gain" belief, but also, with each stretching experience, I've discovered that I'm more confident and stronger.

Whenever I am faced with an opportunity that scares me, I've learned to act fast—to jump right in before the fearful voices start demanding attention.

MULL OVER

If you're someone who practices yoga, you'll be familiar with the idea of a power pose—it's a position or posture that creates a stronger, more assertive stance. In these poses, your arms or legs are extended, your shoulders are back, and your gaze is focused. With each movement, the goal is to increase energy and power throughout your body.

As you develop strength and balance—skills needed to maintain a power pose—you learn to quiet your mind and shift your focus. The focus is particularly important. The secret to maintaining a strong posture is to avoid looking at other people. Most likely, they are moving or swaying in an effort to perfect their own posture. The second you shift your focus and start watching them, you'll lose your balance. You may even fall over.

There's a lesson here. A strong power pose can only be achieved when you are focused fully on yourself—your body, your mind, your energy. Think about what that looks like. A power pose doesn't happen when you lean on other people or prop yourself up on a wall or a desk or some other object. It happens when you're standing tall, with your feet firm and your gaze concentrated on a specific focal point and a specific goal.

Too often, we depend on other people to prop us up, looking to them for support and encouragement. We want them to protect us from uncomfortable experiences. We need them to hold our hands when we're afraid.

But I want to challenge you to get comfortable being uncomfortable. I want you to hold your own hand, like a best friend would when you are afraid or anxious.

What does that mean? So many times, we use being scared as an excuse. And let's face it: no one likes feeling uncomfortable.

But it's in those moments of discomfort that you can grow. You're stretching yourself—and also stretching your concept of who you are and what you can be. As you push those boundaries, you'll discover new areas of strength.

Change isn't easy. But if you're not happy with who you are today, if you're tired of accepting a smaller you, a more fearful you, then you need to welcome that change and recognize that it's not going to feel easy at first.

Please understand: I'm not suggesting that you immediately push yourself into wildly awkward situations! I suppose that can be one way to stretch your boundaries, but I have a different idea. My approach was to try small steps that made me nervous but led to growth and increased my self-confidence. I'll share some of these steps at the end of this chapter. My goal is always to recognize that life is a whirlwind but to develop the skills to control the whirlwind, rather than letting it control me.

Think for a moment about how this applies to your story. What is your fear of being uncomfortable blocking you from trying? Is there a class you'd like to take? A role you'd like to audition for? A job or an internship that seems perfect?

I'VE LEARNED THAT SELF-CONFIDENCE ISN'T A WALL OR A SHIELD THAT BLOCKS NEGATIVE THOUGHTS AND COMMENTS—IT'S A SPRINGBOARD THAT HELPS YOU BOUNCE BACK UP.

I used to think that confidence meant that I wouldn't be unhappy, that other people's criticism wouldn't bother me. But I've learned that self-confidence isn't a wall or a shield that blocks negative thoughts and comments—it's a springboard that helps you bounce back up. You will have setbacks—moments when you're dissatisfied with yourself, moments when someone says or does something that hurts. But as you work through this book, beginning to develop the skills you'll need to feel more confident, to love yourself, you'll find that it gets much easier to get back up and try again.

In those setbacks, and in the moments when you're feeling afraid of being uncomfortable, that's when you need to hold your own hand. Imagine that the brave version of you is reaching out and leading the shy version of you, encouraging you when you hesitate and cheering for you with each small success.

It's a process. This is a journey. Don't let the setbacks define you.

There will be times when fear takes over, and that's OK. You'll grow from those experiences too. Don't waste time beating yourself up—a best friend wouldn't do that. Shift your focus, and start looking for the next opportunity to be a little uncomfortable.

PSYCH OUT

Dr. Martin Seligman is an expert in actions and strategies that build resilience, confidence, and optimism. He's commonly known as the founder of an area of study known as "positive psychology," which examines the strengths that enable people and communities to thrive. Positive psychology is based on the belief that people want to lead meaningful and fulfilling lives and to cultivate what is best within themselves.

Dr. Seligman is especially well known for creating a theory of well-being that's very popular in psychology: the PERMA theory. PERMA is an acronym:

- Positive Emotion

- Engagement

- Relationships

- Meaning and Purpose

- Accomplishments

Let's take a look at each of these five elements. First is *Positive Emotion*. This doesn't just mean a temporary feeling of positivity; it's a deeper ability to be optimistic and to look at your past, your present, and your future constructively, recognizing that not everything will be good or easy, but that each experience brings lessons that will help you grow. As a part of becoming your own best friend, you want to be able to bring Positive Emotion to how you interact with yourself. Think about how a best friend would be optimistic and supportive and would remind you that they are there to help you. Then try to incorporate those things into how you treat yourself, as your own best friend.

Engagement means doing something that you love. It might be a sport, or singing, or spending time outdoors, or volunteering. It's those activities that you can't wait to do, the ones where you lose all track of time.

Relationships are also key to well-being. This is a challenging concept to those of us struggling to find a group where we fit in, but the science shows that pain centers in the human brain are triggered when we're isolated. We need these connections to others, but the relationships don't refer only to peers. It can be family, a club, or a group that shares your values or beliefs.

Thinking about *Meaning and Purpose* can feel daunting, but it's another building block for well-being. You may not be able to answer the question "Why am I here?" today, but that doesn't mean that you can't begin to live your life in a way that equips you to respond in the future. Reflecting on ways to make a difference in your community is a great starting point. Volunteering for a good cause, helping to care for a sick friend or family member, expressing yourself creatively, or diving deeper into religion or spirituality are all ways to develop this element of your own well-being.

Finally, and not surprisingly, having goals matters. That's what the *Accomplishments* element represents. You need goals to strive for—goals that are realistic and achievable. Goals give you targets to work toward, and as we talked about earlier, when you push yourself and then achieve those goals, you end up with a sense of pride and accomplishment.

In the PERMA theory, Dr. Seligman distinguishes well-being

from happiness. I believe this is an important point, one that reflects the focus of this chapter. Each of the elements in his theory—Positive Emotion, Engagement, Relationships, Meaning and Purpose, and Accomplishments—may require a certain amount of discomfort, especially at the beginning. True well-being occurs, according to Dr. Seligman, "when your highest strengths are deployed to meet the highest challenges that come your way."[2]

Cultivating habits that will enhance your confidence is one path to well-being. It's also good for your health. In one study from the Netherlands, researchers reported that students with higher self-esteem performed better in school, and that adults with higher levels of self-esteem reported greater job satisfaction later in life. Self-esteem is also strongly linked to happiness, with higher levels of self-esteem predicting greater levels of happiness. High self-confidence has even been found to increase the chances of survival after a serious surgical procedure.[3]

POWER UP

The science is clear. Developing a certain amount of comfort in uncomfortable situations, taking steps to increase your self-confidence, will have both short- and long-term benefits.

So what can you do? What techniques can you use today to stretch yourself, challenge yourself, and ultimately boost your self-confidence?

First of all, take a moment to do a quick self-assessment. When I

---

2   Martin Seligman, "Authentic Happiness," April 2011, https://www.authentichappiness.sas.upenn.edu/learn/wellbeing.

3   Michal Mann et al., "Self-esteem in a broad-spectrum approach for mental health promotion," *Health Education Research* 19, no. 4, 357–372 (2004), https://academic.oup.com/her/article/19/4/357/560320.

talk about doing something that makes you feel uncomfortable, what comes to mind? Is there a goal hidden in that fear, an activity or an action that you wish you had the confidence to try?

Take a moment and picture yourself pushing into that uncomfortable space. Imagine what you are doing or saying there. Admit that it feels uncomfortable, but also think about what else you might be feeling. Excited? Energized? Embarrassed? Now picture that brave version of you—the one who has chosen to not let fear be a barrier—holding your hand. What is that brave self saying to you?

I know that courage and self-confidence don't appear magically when you try something new. My message is to take one small step. It's a journey, yes, but you don't have to go the full distance today.

I suggest writing a goal list for yourself, and start with at least three simple goals. Make them small and realistic—you want to check them off your list!

If you're like me when I started this journey—quiet, shy—your goals might be to raise your hand in class or talk to the person behind the counter when you get lunch or the barista at your favorite coffee shop. You don't have to have a five-minute conversation; just ask them how their day is going. Another good starting point is to say hi to random people on the street—not like a crazy person, but as if you are being neighborly. The stakes are low—they're just strangers, people you're only passing for a few seconds, so if they don't respond, well, you're probably never going to see them again. But the payoff is that you'll begin to increase your confidence when it comes to social situations and interacting with new people.

If this doesn't feel like a stretch, then your goals should be a bit more ambitious. Maybe you want to try striking up a conversation with the classmate or coworker you'd like to be friends with. Or your goal can be to compliment at least five people every day.

Under each goal, make a note of the opportunities you'll have to practice this exercise or fulfill this goal. Once it's accomplished, check it off and allow yourself to feel proud! You've taken another step on your path toward growth and positive change.

To give you an idea of what I mean, this is what my goals might look like for the week:

Overall goal: I want to feel confident in my social skills.

Goals for this week:

- Say hi to at least five people I haven't spoken to yet.

- *Opportunities*: School, work, on the walk back from school, gym, golf course, library

- Strike up one conversation with that one classmate I want to be friends with.

- *Opportunities*: Lunchtime at school, in between classes

- Compliment at least five people every day.

- *Opportunities*: School, work, on the walk back from school, gym, golf course, library

- Ask the person behind the counter how their day is.

- *Opportunities*: Morning when I get coffee, lunchtime, when I pick up takeout food, gym

CONVINCING YOURSELF TO GET STARTED MAY BE THE HARDEST CHALLENGE YOU FACE.

I know that change feels uncomfortable. I understand that you may not be feeling brave or confident.

I've been exactly where you are. And I can tell you that it's definitely worth it to push yourself, to challenge yourself, to begin the process of becoming your own best support system. Convincing yourself to get started may be the hardest challenge you face.

Set your goals and prove to yourself that you are capable. Don't be afraid of feeling uncomfortable, because your best friend (you!) will be there to hold your hand.

NOTES

_____

_____

_____

_____

_____

_____

_____

_____

_____

_____

_____

_____

_____

_____

_____

_____

_____

_____

CHAPTER THREE

Confront Your Strengths and Weaknesses

Knowing others is intelligence. Knowing yourself is true wisdom.
Mastering others is strength. Mastering yourself is true power.

—LAO TZU

I am a strong person. My strength comes from a solid pillar of independence. I believe in the importance of friends and family, but I've learned to be self-reliant, and that ability to be self-sustaining has helped me through some challenging situations.

I'm not afraid of testing myself, of placing myself in circumstances where I might not immediately feel strong or confident. I've learned to be OK with those moments when I have to feel weak before I can feel strong again. I want to change and grow, even if that means I have to build a new skill or acknowledge a problem and take steps to correct it.

DROP IN

I'm going to ask you a question that pops up all the time on job applications and interviews: What is your greatest strength?

I know. It's hard to step back and assess yourself neutrally without sounding like you're bragging, but this is an opportunity to practice some of the techniques we talked about earlier. So think for a moment about the things you do well, the skills that come naturally, and the growth you're working hard to achieve.

Now: What is your greatest strength?

I asked this question of Susan RoAne. She's an expert at business networking and the author of *How to Work a Room*. Susan says that her greatest strength is her ability to build relationships. This comes from staying in touch with people she likes, following up, and following through.

As Susan points out, you don't always know ahead of time who the "right people" are to talk to. A relationship that you build today may impact your success months, or even years, later. But as Susan says, "You earn opportunity through relationships."

I've been doing a lot of self-reflecting lately as I write this book and as I prepare to apply to college. I've realized that my greatest strength is this: I don't like to be normal.

Dr. Seuss's quote "Why fit in when you were born to stand out?" is a perfect reflection of how I feel. I've often wondered why so many people waste so much time trying to fit in instead of celebrating what makes them special and unique. I'm someone who is very conscious about how I spend my time and how to most efficiently spend it to achieve my goals. If you keep giving time to something that won't serve you, you're wasting precious time that could be spent building a skill or taking another step for your career.

I see it all the time, and you probably do too: the celebrity whom everyone is imitating; the pretty, popular girl whose style others immediately copy. I don't understand the idea of trying to squeeze yourself into someone else's box. Why imitate someone else when you can spend that time developing your unique self? If, as discussed in chapter one, you know who you are and who you want to become, why would you try to be like anybody else?

I'VE OFTEN WONDERED WHY SO MANY PEOPLE WASTE SO MUCH TIME TRYING TO FIT IN INSTEAD OF CELEBRATING WHAT MAKES THEM SPECIAL AND UNIQUE.

Being your authentic self sends a strong message to those around you: the genuine you is worthy of being showcased to the world.

I'm not saying that it is wrong to want to emulate someone you admire. Rather, I am encouraging you to assess whether your desire to emulate these people is healthy. I know people who have become anorexic or who are obsessed with spending money in an effort to become the person they admire—this is not the kind of behavior you want to adopt.

MULL OVER

Let's reflect on the idea of "strengths" and "weaknesses." For some people, "strengths" refer to something physical—the ability to demonstrate real strength in a concrete way, maybe by lifting heavy weights. For others, there's an emotional element—you are "strong" if you don't let your feelings show, if you don't cry, if you ignore criticism from others. You may be someone who thinks about strengths and weaknesses in terms of academics or professional accomplishments.

I don't think there's a right or wrong way to view this. My suggestion is to reflect on what matters only to you. When I ask you to identify your strengths and weaknesses, the areas that come to mind reveal a bit about what you value right now, at this moment in your life, and that's OK.

They also give you a useful road map of the goals you'd like to tackle when it comes to personal growth. That's the purpose of this chapter—to honestly confront your strengths and weaknesses and use that knowledge as a springboard and a resource to help you achieve growth.

What does addressing your strengths and weaknesses look like? I like making something similar to a to-do list. I take a moment to honestly identify what I do well, and where I'd like to see growth and improvement. Then, I do a brain dump and just write all of my thoughts on a piece of paper or on my phone. The purpose is to acknowledge what I've already accomplished and what remains to be done. This enables me to sift through my list to pinpoint the traits or characteristics that are impacting my life negatively—the ones I want to address immediately.

You can do this too. It's not simply a matter of identifying weaknesses. You want to prioritize them so that you can take steps to address them.

In the past, I've worked on one weakness that I identified: getting more comfortable in social situations. Acknowledging this weakness, identifying it, and admitting that it has impacted my life has meant that I could then begin to think about steps to take to develop that comfort.

Perhaps you, like I did during lunch at one point, feel pressure to act and look like the people around you. If this sounds like you, check out the Peer Pressure box to read what I have to say about peer pressure and the urge to conform.

Peer Pressure

In my experience as a high schooler who doesn't drink or do drugs, I definitely felt like an outsider, especially when others would ask me if I wanted to smoke or drink a beer. My go-to answer to "Do you drink? Do you smoke?" would be "It's honestly none of my business if others do that, but I don't."

At first, I felt uncomfortable sharing that I didn't drink or do drugs, but over time, I felt more confident saying that because I noticed that people respected my decision and actually started opening up to me more about their experience. People felt more comfortable being honest around me because they saw that I was unafraid of standing by my beliefs, and I didn't judge others for what they decided to do. In fact, the people who would ask me these things would then start sharing things like "Oh, yeah, I actually only smoked weed once at a party and hated it" or talk about how they just drink water out of a red Solo cup and pretend to be drunk at parties.

I believe that you can use exercises and techniques to address any kind of weakness or limitation. It's funny; I think we're much more comfortable acknowledging that we're working on physical weaknesses than on other kinds of limitations. It's not a big deal to tell a friend that you're trying some new techniques to run faster, improve your golf swing, or develop more endurance. So why should it be different to admit that you're trying some exercises, investing time, even seeking some outside expert advice to address other weaknesses—to stop comparing yourself to other people, or to speak up in class or in meetings? Why are we more comfortable acknowledging that we're trying to manage physical strengths and weaknesses than weaknesses in any other areas?

I think it's about perception. While we may be willing to admit external strengths and weaknesses—those that impact our body— we're more hesitant to admit the internal strengths and weaknesses that are impacting our thoughts. It's much easier to say to a friend, "Hey, I've got this new exercise routine I'm trying," than to say, "Hey, I'm working on becoming more of a self-starter by listing my weaknesses today."

It may be helpful to think about this process like taking a car in for servicing. The mechanic may check the systems in your car and then let you know what needs to be repaired or replaced. Some of these repairs may be more urgent—things that will prevent you from being able to safely and comfortably drive the car. Others may be something that you'll need to think about in the future but aren't priorities right now.

If you can bring that same neutral approach to assessing your strengths and weaknesses, it will make it easier to decide where to focus your energy. Remember, the goal is not to be overly critical of yourself. Your goal is growth. Be your own best friend when doing this, and be objective in your assessment. Are there certain weaknesses on your list that you need to tackle immediately, the ones that are holding you back and impacting you today? Those should be your priorities.

PSYCH OUT

It's challenging to honestly assess your strengths and weaknesses. Research suggests that it's even harder for women than men.

One Cornell University study found that men overestimate their abilities and performance, while women underestimate both. In the study, female students rated their ability lower than men, though their performance was almost the same—the female students got 7.5 out of 10 questions correct, while the male students answered 7.9 questions correctly.[4]

It's interesting to consider how the ability to do necessary self-assessment also impacts future career choices. One Hewlett-Packard report showed that men will apply for a job or promotion when they meet only 60 percent of the qualifications, but women won't apply unless they meet 100 percent of the qualifications.[5]

The inability to accurately identify your weaknesses impacts even the most successful women. Consider tech entrepreneur Clara Shih, who founded the social media company Hearsay Social and joined the Starbucks board when she was only twenty-nine. As a college student at Stanford, she was convinced that all of the other students found the computer science courses much easier than she did. She ended up graduating with the highest GPA of any computer science major in her class.[6]

As these studies show, women in particular are likely to struggle

---

4   Katty Kay and Claire Shipman, "The confidence gap," *The Atlantic*, https://www.theatlantic.com/magazine/archive/2014/05/the-confidence-gap/359815/.

5   Jack Zenger, "The confidence gap in men and women," *Forbes*, https://www.forbes.com/sites/jackzenger/2018/04/08/the-confidence-gap-in-men-and-women-why-it-matters-and-how-to-overcome-it/#4e273a223bfa.

6   Kay and Shipman, op cit.

with accurate self-assessment. I think we all find it easier to quickly identify weaknesses, while we are much slower to acknowledge our strengths.

I talked about the value of self-assessment earlier in this book, and this is another area where that kind of knowledge and understanding is helpful. As you work through tests like those I recommended in chapter one, you can use your results to better identify your strengths and weaknesses and more objectively consider potential growth areas.

> THERE IS POWER IN POSITIVE SELF-ASSESSMENT—POWER THAT YOU CAN USE TO IMPROVE THE QUALITY OF YOUR LIFE.

There is power in positive self-assessment—power that you can use to improve the quality of your life. When you spend time assessing your behaviors, thoughts, and experiences carefully and neutrally, you will find it easier to make positive change.

POWER UP

Before I end this chapter, I want to encourage you to do more than simply identify your strengths and weaknesses. I don't want you to focus too much on the idea of what's "good" and "bad" and lose sight of how you can use this knowledge to build realistic new skills.

It's not a matter of "This is what I don't like about myself." Instead, it should be "This is what is working, and this is what needs improvement so that I can function more efficiently and reach my goals faster."

Try to detach yourself from the emotion that can creep in when you're focused on self-improvement. Imagine that you are giving feedback to a friend or coworker. Always start with well-earned praise ("This is where I'm showing growth") and include some constructive criticism ("These are some areas where I'd like to improve").

To practice this skill, identify three strengths—areas where you've shown growth—and three weaknesses, places where you want to focus some energy and time. After each strength or weakness, ask yourself a "Why?" question about that specific characteristic. "Why am I confident in my abilities in this area?" "Why does this specific skill matter to me today?"

The "Why?" questions are important—they will help you uncover the roots of what's challenging you, as well as the foundations that have led to growth. Don't be afraid to dig deep and to think clearly about what you are feeling. Remember that you are identifying and exercising the skills you'll need to achieve your goals.

Once you feel comfortable asking yourself these kinds of questions, try increasing the degree of difficulty by adding a new set of questions.

By asking yourself "Why?" you've identified the skills that matter to you. Your next step is to ask yourself "How?" "How am I going to exercise this skill?" This is where you begin to create a road map of steps you'll need to take.

Remember, you've spent time considering your strengths and weaknesses to get closer to your goals, whether professional or personal. The "How?" questions show you what's next, the concrete steps that will lead you forward to those goals.

NOTES

CHAPTER FOUR

Build Your Support Network

Be strong enough to stand alone, smart enough to know
when you need help, and brave enough to ask for it.
—ZIAD K. ABDELNOUR

M y focus in the first chapters of this book has been on self-discovery and confidence. I wanted to share techniques that have helped me believe in myself and develop the inner strength I use to push through challenges and setbacks.

When I started on my journey of growth and self-development, my goal was to be so strong that I didn't need other people. I wanted to be enough—to be able to rely on myself without needing support from anyone else. I went so far as to believe that if I received support from others, that made me weak because that meant I couldn't solely support myself.

But I've learned that the strongest people don't get all of their strength from themselves; they also get it from other people. A strong support network can be a key resource for encouragement and empowerment, and it can fill gaps in your life that you would not be able to identify and resolve on your own.

In this chapter, we'll consider how to identify and develop that critical external source of support. I want to help you build relationships that empower you while encouraging you to continue to practice the techniques that hone your inner strength. Though I do believe that inner strength should be the biggest support pillar in your life, it is important to have supplemental support systems to keep you standing strong. Remember to be your own best friend, but also remember that your best friend needs allies who will support and encourage you as much as your best friend does.

DROP IN

I'm a classic Type A personality.

You've probably heard this before—someone describes themselves, or someone else, as "Type A." In case you've wondered what this means, I'll give a quick explanation.

Psychologists sometimes group people into four broad personality types to help clarify differences in the way humans approach work or school, social situations, problem solving, and risk taking. It's a method of analysis to understand why some people will jump at the chance to learn a new language or interact with new people and others prefer to methodically work their way through a task or are more comfortable supporting rather than leading a group project.

The basic idea is that people broadly fall into four types based on orientation—they tend to be goal oriented, relationship oriented, detail oriented, or task oriented. There are different terms used for these four types. Sometimes you'll see them listed as the Director, the Socializer, the Thinker, and the Supporter. But most commonly they are referred to by letters: Type A, Type B, Type C, and Type D.

So when I describe myself as a classic Type A personality, what do I mean? Well, I'm ambitious and passionate about my goals. I like to take charge in challenging situations and work at a fast pace. I'm competitive. But like other Type As, I can be stubborn and impatient. I like to be in control.

I've been thinking about this lately—the interesting dynamic between strength and control. It's tempting to think that strength comes from being in control, but as we discussed in the previous chapters, part of the benefit of developing inner strength and confidence is the ability to navigate times when you're not in control.

It's a point I'd like to stress here. Just because I encourage you to be your own best support system doesn't mean that you should be your only source of support. You need other people—mentors and role models, but also a network of people of many different ages and backgrounds who encourage you.

No matter your personality type, it's important to consider how you interact and build your support network. If you're a Type B personality, you're outgoing and

YOU NEED OTHER PEOPLE—MENTORS AND ROLE MODELS, BUT ALSO A NETWORK OF PEOPLE OF MANY DIFFERENT AGES AND BACKGROUNDS WHO ENCOURAGE YOU.

derive energy from being around other people. It may seem as if that's a personality type that will definitely have a strong support network, but Type B people crave approval from others and may find it challenging to build the kind of relationships that generate honest, sometimes critical, feedback. Type C personalities are thinkers—logical and detail oriented. When you're that analytical, it can be challenging to interact with unpredictable people, so you'll need to make sure to prioritize building the kind of relationships that foster a good support system. If you're a Type D, you're more easygoing, calm, low key—the kind of person who wants to get along with others. But you'll need to be thoughtful as you build your support system; your challenge will be to get comfortable with trustworthy people who may sometimes deliver uncomfortable truths.

Let's be honest: relationships can be messy and unpredictable. For someone like me, who likes to have a significant amount of control over her world, letting other people into that environment can feel risky.

I had a friend—I'll call her Sara. We were very close, but whenever there was a hiccup in our friendship because of a disagreement or misunderstanding or something else, it made me sad or anxious. It was uncomfortable—that sense of not being in control of my feelings. I began to believe that it was a weakness, a sign that I was relying on other people for my well-being and happiness.

I'm sure that being bullied played a role in this as well. I was trying to develop a tougher exterior so that other people's words and actions wouldn't negatively impact my life, but that desire to be tough led me to make choices designed to protect me from being in a position where I was vulnerable—I began to isolate myself. I started unconsciously pushing people away, avoiding old friends and opportunities to make new ones as a form of self-protection.

I developed the idea that self-confidence and empowerment meant that you didn't need anybody else. Because the only person I could fully control was myself, I began to avoid relationships with other people.

I was wrong.

There were three main events that led to my taking the initiative to change how I viewed support from others. At my old school, I often chose to sit alone in the library so I could finish my homework. I found this to be the most practical, useful way to spend my time, but as I went to class and had conversations with my friends

BECAUSE THE ONLY PERSON I COULD FULLY CONTROL WAS MYSELF, I BEGAN TO AVOID RELATIONSHIPS WITH OTHER PEOPLE. I WAS WRONG.

after school, I realized how distant we were becoming. When I transferred high schools, I felt most comfortable being by myself because that's what I had trained myself to do. Some people at my new school would ask me whom I would hang out with after school or whom I would sit with at lunch, and I had no answers. The third event is more recent. I'm writing this book during the COVID-19 pandemic, when quarantines, school closures, and social distancing have been normal. Toward the beginning of the COVID-19 quarantine, I felt really alone and missed daily interactions with people at school. This is when I realized the true importance of relationships with others (for physical and mental health) and made an actual effort to reconnect with lost friends and make new ones.

I want to encourage you to value your relationships with others and to identify and develop relationships with the people who can be your support network.

There's a mindfulness that's important here. It's not simply a matter of positioning yourself in the middle of a crowd. You want to be thoughtful about the people you surround yourself with—not because of an ambitious desire to be part of some nebulous elite, but because your support network should be made of people who encourage you to be your best, lend a helping hand, and redirect you when you veer off track.

MULL OVER

I've talked a lot about power and strength in this book, but I want to pause here and reflect on the idea of *wholesome support*.

Let's first look at the definition of the word *support*. There's the idea of lifting something up, like a prop or a foundation. A support can also be an advocate—someone who acts in your interests or argues in your favor. And finally, there's the concept of sustaining something or someone—preventing them from falling or giving up, encouraging them to keep going.

When you think about building your support network, I urge you to keep all of these definitions in mind. You want to surround yourself with people who lift you up and make you feel encouraged. You want to surround yourself with people who will fight for you and promote you to others. You also want to surround yourself with people who will tell you when you are wrong and help you recover from your mistakes. You don't necessarily want everyone around you to make you feel good all the time, because that isn't in your best interest.

It can be hard to identify the people who will support you. It's not always easy to see the difference between true friends and acquaintances. Building relationships with those who will be true friends involves the idea of "being comfortable being uncomfortable" because true friends will criticize you and tell you when you are wrong.

Below are my *Six Types of Acquaintances*. These are six types of people that belong in the "acquaintance" category. You probably know people who fit into each of these types! Understand that I'm not telling you to push them away; just know that you shouldn't expect more from them than they can deliver. They may be fun to spend time with, but they won't be part of your support network. When you take a look at this list, make sure that you aren't being one of these people either!

Six Types of Acquaintances

The Flakes: People who don't follow through on what they say. Flakes may make you feel like you're the reason why things aren't moving, when in reality they are the problem. Relying on these types of people to get your plans to move forward is a waste of time and energy. It gets tiring to try to make something happen with someone who has no intention of making it happen. You don't need another person to push when pushing yourself can be challenging enough.

The Lazies: People who are not dedicated to bettering themselves. Lazies are unmotivated and don't want more for themselves. You don't want to expect that they will help you grow; they have never grown themselves. It can be very unmotivating and draining being around people like this. The Lazies can also suck the energy out of you or try to deflate your ideas about moving forward toward success. They may do this to make themselves feel better, as they like to see others who are also lazy to justify being lazy themselves. The Lazies can also sometimes overlap with the Tear Downs or the Pushers. At the beginning of your journey of self-development, you may have surrounded yourself with people like the Lazies, because they were those who you were most comfortable around—they don't want more for you, and you don't want more for them. These are the types of people I was friends with at the start of my journey of change. As you start to grow, however, I would advise you to reevaluate your support network and make sure there aren't any of the Lazies in there, as they won't help you achieve your goals.

 The Pleasers: People who are looking to make you feel good all of the time. These people are not acting in your best interest because they just want you to like them. You want people in your support network who will give you constructive criticism and tell you when you are wrong. The Pleasers' motivations for wanting you to like them most likely stem from wanting something out of associating with you, whether that's increased social status, homework help, or so on. Though you may enjoy their company because they try to please you, you can't learn from someone who is simply trying to make you feel good. It's not necessarily bad to accept these people's compliments, but just keep in mind that they may not always be genuine.

The Tear Downs: People who just want to bring you down. These people make you feel like you aren't good enough; they don't want to see you succeed. They don't have a positive self-image or real self-confidence, so criticizing other people makes them feel superior. They bring no value to your life. I would like to point out here that there is a difference between constructive criticism and words meant to tear you down. The former is given with the intention to help you grow, while the latter is given with the intention to make you feel bad and lose confidence—in effect, stopping your personal growth.

The Pressurers: People who try to encourage you to adopt their bad habits or unhealthy behaviors. These people typically try to get you to do something they do that isn't healthy, whether it's negative self-talk, criticism of everything, drugs—anything to make them feel less alone in their bad habits. Pressurers will make you feel bad for the way you live your life or for sticking to your values if they clash with what the Pressurer wants you to do. This is classic peer pressure behavior and is something you should learn to recognize and feel confident avoiding.

 The Unavailables: People whom you admire or are successful but who aren't willing to help you get to where they are. Not everyone is going to help you out. That's another reason why I wanted to write this book and to share what I've learned with you. It's important to remember that there are some successful people who simply don't have the time to help. Don't be discouraged when you reach out to them; just understand and move on.

When you began this chapter and saw that its focus was on building your support network, a picture of what that looked like may have come immediately to mind. But I'm encouraging you not to get too caught up in an image or an ideal. Don't waste time writing a script that doesn't fit your story.

Your support network may not look like you think it should or like anyone else's. Your support network should be a unique reflection of who you are.

When I started high school, I had a clear picture of what my support network should look like: a big group of my peers, other high school girls. We would all love each other and be great friends and help each other survive the next four years.

That's definitely not how it turned out.

I was at a different school than my friends from middle school. And it wasn't just the students who were different. The culture was also very different from what I had known in middle school—it was much more focused on academics, and there was a clear difference between students who were in the gifted program and those, like me, who weren't.

I then transferred to a different high school, where I had to go through another culture shock, coming from an academically focused school and transferring to a school run by cliques and sports. This time, it was worse because I transferred in the middle of high school, when people had already solidified their friend groups.

Because of these things, there was never a place at school that I easily fit into; instead, I found that I made friends more easily with the older kids at school. I liked being friends with older students because they gave me advice on college, classes to take, and the best teachers. They were also a more wholesome source of support compared to my peers who were the same age as me because my older friends and I weren't competing with each other to get into top universities.

That's why my support network looks different from how I expected. Since I couldn't find a group of friends among people my age at school, I looked to other places to fill that need for external support.

In chapter one, we talked a bit about reframing experiences and expectations. That skill is extremely useful when it comes to building your support network. This is a good time to check in with yourself to make sure that you're considering your network carefully, assessing it to ensure that it's a source of healthy support.

I'm fortunate that my family is a key part of that healthy support. I'm lucky to have a great relationship with my mom and dad and brother. Even my dog is a source of healthy support. That may sound funny—a pet as part of your support network—but the National Institutes of Health have studied the power of pets and found that interacting with animals can decrease levels of cortisol (a stress-related hormone) and lower blood pressure; pets can also boost your mood, increase feelings of social support, and reduce loneliness.[7] So, yes, pets can be part of your support network!

But let me talk for a minute about other unexpected sources of support—the ones you'll want to look for to help build your network. Last summer, I took a job as a tutor. That job had two parts—I served as a calculus tutor to several college students, and I also taught English to two children who had just moved to the United States from Korea.

It's the second part of my tutoring job that led to an unexpected source of support. Those two little children—their names were Lucy and C. J.—were ferociously determined in their efforts to learn English. Everything was new to them—new language, new country, new home—but their dedication to mastering English was amazing. Every time I met with Lucy and C. J., they inspired me. They weren't consciously trying to motivate me, of course, but their attitude was contagious. I was motivated because of their motivation. I left those tutoring sessions feeling very happy and very positive, and they became part of my support network. I even wrote in my school planner, "If Lucy and C. J. can do it, so can I." This little reminder helped me do my best when studying for school tests.

---

7   NIH News in Health, "The Power of Pets," February 2018, https://newsin-health.nih.gov/sites/nihNIH/files/2018/February/NIHNiHFeb2018.pdf.

Too often, we get distracted by an idea of the most stereotypical sources of support—friends, family—and miss the very real possibilities in the people around us. You may believe that sources of support have to be peers, or someone older with knowledge and experience you don't have. But that's not necessarily true. I found support, encouragement, and motivation from two children much younger than me. It was authentic support, without feelings of competition or unrealistic expectations.

So how can you identify a good, wholesome source of support? First, when you spend time with your support network, you should feel lifted up in some way. Wholesome support comes from people you can be authentic with—you don't have to pretend to be someone else. When I left my sessions with C. J. and Lucy, I felt energized. That's a good sign that you've found a source of support.

I believe that the people in your network can serve different purposes, providing precisely the kinds of support you need. For example, Lucy and C. J. helped motivate me and inspired me with their positive outlook and determination to learn new skills. Another person in my support network is someone I play golf with. He helps inspire me to continue to perfect my golf game and reassures me on those days when my swing is off or my shots end up in all the wrong places. My family provides a kind of grounding—I can go home and find relief from the stress of school and experience gratitude for the things that are going well. I also find support in a few friends who are in college—they inspire me and help me stay focused on my longer-term goals.

It's a broad network, with people of different ages and backgrounds. They all bring different pieces to the puzzle. All of these people in my support network satisfy a different need of mine, whether that need is a smaller one or a critical one. By satisfying these needs, they help me live a fuller, happier life. I also want to point out that those in your support network may not necessarily consider you as a member of their support network. Take Lucy and C. J., for example. I considered them as a part of my support network, but to them, I was just their tutor. And that's OK.

I'd also like to make note that your support network will shift and evolve as your needs and goals change. Because your support network helps you satisfy your needs and pushes you closer to achieving your goals, it is natural for the network to change as what you need changes.

I've spoken a lot about how those in your support network can help satisfy your needs and encourage you toward your goals, but remember to reciprocate. You want the relationships that you build with those in your support network to be healthy, well-balanced exchanges. You don't want to keep taking without giving, because then the relationships you build won't be wholesome; they'll be one sided.

PSYCH OUT

I talked earlier about how the positive attitudes of Lucy and C. J. were contagious. There's scientific research to support this idea that strong, wholesome relationships matter.

Will Meek, a psychologist at Washington State University, says that a support network is vital to a healthy life. "When we lack stable and supportive relationships," he explains, "we can become depressed and anxious."[8]

I used the term "healthy sources of support" in this chapter, and that's an important distinction. Much like a healthy diet promotes

---

8   Elizabeth Svoboda, "Lessons for Living," *Psychology Today*, September 3, 2012, https://www.psychologytoday.com/us/articles/201209/lessons-living.

physical strength and well-being, the same is true of healthy relationships. You'll want to avoid the quick and easy, fast-food-type connections—the types I described as acquaintances—formed just because of proximity and maybe because they look appealing at first glance. I don't mean to suggest that some people are the equivalent of junk food, but let's face it: we've all spent time with someone who wasn't what they seemed to be, who wasn't good for us. My encouragement to you is to take the extra time to look for healthier alternatives.

LET'S FACE IT: WE'VE ALL SPENT TIME WITH SOMEONE WHO WASN'T WHAT THEY SEEMED TO BE, WHO WASN'T GOOD FOR US. MY ENCOURAGEMENT TO YOU IS TO TAKE THE EXTRA TIME TO LOOK FOR HEALTHIER ALTERNATIVES.

Burt Uchino, a psychologist at the University of Utah, discovered that more robust and healthier relationships can improve heart health and in fact help you to live longer. His research has shown that individuals with fewer sources of wholesome social support had increased mortality rates; the evidence showed that the risks of poor health and even death in people who lacked support networks were as compelling as risk factors such as smoking and lack of physical activity.[9]

Uchino's research is significant because it focused not just on the quantity of connections you have, but on their quality—and the quality of these relationships matters. In one study, he recorded the blood pressure of eighty-eight women in a stressful situation—they were preparing to give a speech. He found that the readings spiked less when a close friend was available to offer participants encourage-

---

9   Burt Uchino, Department of Psychology, University of Utah, https://psych.utah.edu/people/faculty/uchino-bert.php.

ment than when they were with a friend who they believed was less supportive. What does this show? One possibility is that a genuine support network may have a protective effect on your cardiovascular system, especially when you're feeling anxious.[10]

And it's not just heart health. There's also interesting research that shows that wholesome support networks can help you fight infections. A team at Carnegie Mellon University studied how social support can protect you from increased susceptibility to colds and other viruses. More than four hundred people were questioned about their sources of social support and then intentionally exposed to a common cold virus and monitored in quarantine to assess infection and symptoms of illness. Among the infected people, greater perceived social support resulted in less severe illness symptoms.[11]

POWER UP

In a discussion about building your support network, I think it's important to include an acknowledgment of the importance of mentors. When you're looking for a job or an internship, when you need career or school advice, mentors can be invaluable. Mentors may not necessarily be connected to a career or profession. Sometimes they are someone who has skills you'd like to develop or an approach to life you'd like to emulate.

I encourage you to identify a mentor and include them in your support network. Find someone whose career path inspires you or who has a skill or talent you are trying to develop. If they seem

---

10 Svoboda, op cit.

11 Shilo Rea, "Hugs Help Protect against Stress and Infection, Say Carnegie Mellon Researchers," Carnegie Mellon University News, December 17, 2014, https://www.cmu.edu/news/stories/archives/2014/december/december17_hugsprotect.html.

approachable, if you have an opportunity to introduce yourself and make a connection, then don't waste that opportunity!

We all love to feel that we are good at something—that we have an area of knowledge or expertise that can be shared. Most people will be flattered if you ask them for advice. Don't take up too much of their time, of course, but ask a quick question that will communicate your interest.

I love to play golf, and I occasionally meet someone who has a technique I admire or who is simply a little bit better at the game. If they have a minute, I might ask them if they'd be willing to look at my swing. If they agree, or if they share some other specific piece of golfing advice, I always pull out my phone and start taking notes while they're talking. It's a way of showing them that I respect them enough to write down what they're saying—I want to keep their advice. It's funny—that also prompts them to keep talking and give me even more advice. It's a win-win situation.

Not every person you approach in this way will end up as part of your support network. But the process of learning how to cultivate those relationships is a vital skill.

Think for a moment about whom you might approach in this way. Do you know someone who has a skill you'd like to develop? Someone who has landed an internship you'd like to apply for in the future, or who is excelling at a class you'll be taking next year, or who has perfected a sport or an instrument or a language that you're just starting to learn?

Consider asking them if they'd be willing to answer a question— just one, remember! You don't want to bombard them or take up too much of their time. Often that first question will lead to an opportunity to ask more. But start with a small step.

If you don't feel ready to reach out in this way, then you may want to first focus on building your support network from the base up. Think about the discussion of healthy sources of support, and identify who comes to mind. You'll want your base to contain authentic relationships, people (and pets!) who are OK with you being yourself. These are the relationships that strengthen you, that encourage you, and that make you feel better just by spending time with them. They may be family or friends. They may be older or younger. Identify those relationships, and spend some time cultivating them. That means prioritizing time with your network, listening, and inviting advice. Assess your network periodically to make sure that you're cultivating healthy relationships and that these connections are helping you to grow.

Be open to looking for small sources of external support every day. It might be a stranger smiling at you as you walk past, or someone giving you a compliment when you perform a task or assignment well. Keep your eyes open for new outlets and new relationships to tap into as you build your support network!

I talked earlier about taking notes when people share valuable advice, and I think there's a real importance in that idea of preserving messages and inspiration. That's another way that I build my support network, and it's something I encourage you to do.

I keep a stash of "letters"—cards and messages and even Post-its that I collect and save. They are a resource when I need encouragement and inspiration, when I'm feeling down and need to remember that there are people who care about me and have my back.

I challenge you to start building your own stash of letters. If you get a birthday card with a message that inspires you, save it. If a teacher writes an encouraging message on a paper, or in your yearbook, tear out that page and keep it. If you get a text from a friend that talks about how much they value your relationship, take a screen shot and save it.

I store up these messages and keep them for those times when I need a reminder from my support network. My system isn't fancy or high tech. Sometimes I print the messages and stick them on a bulletin board or tape them to a wall. Other messages I print out and clip together, putting them in a drawer until I need them. When I feel like I need some extra love, I open up my drawer and pull out those clipped letters and messages.

I put Post-it notes on some of them that describe the contents. One might say, "Read this when you feel like you're not good enough." Another Post-it note might say, "Read this when you want to look over how far you've come." My letters date back for several years and continue to encourage me long after the original message was sent.

Surround yourself with these reminders of your support network. Use pictures, envelopes, notes, and drawings—whatever visual sign you need. Tape them next to your bed so you see them when you fall asleep at night and when you wake up in the morning. Paste them by a mirror. When you surround yourself with positive messages like this, you'll find encouragement from your support network, no matter where you look.

NOTES

CHAPTER FIVE

Success Is the Best Revenge

I don't gotta get revenge. My life does that enough.
—RUSS

'm motivated by a drive to be successful in many different areas. If you're reading this, I'm sure you are too.

Success is tricky to measure and comes in different shapes and sizes. For some of us, it may be improving your GPA or finally grasping a tricky math concept. For others, it may be being accepted into a good college, or earning a spot on the varsity team, or being hired for a job or internship.

I'm a big believer in setting goals and working to achieve success. For a while, I'll admit, part of that drive was based on a desire to prove myself—to the people who doubted me, who bullied me, who ignored me.

It's not necessarily wrong or bad to be motivated by revenge, by a desire to show those who tried to dismiss you who you really are and what you actually are capable of achieving. But it's not a sustainable or ideal source of motivation. It's a goal that is too dependent on someone else's behavior or responses to your actions. Your main source of motivation should always be something that you can control.

In this chapter, we'll look at success as a way to live well. My hope is that you'll start to plan your goals, your path to success, in sustainable ways that empower you. We'll focus not so much on getting revenge, but instead on taking actions that will fulfill you, using sources of motivation that you can control. If you want to consider it in terms of revenge, think about getting revenge on the part of you that didn't want the best for you, the part that kept dragging you down.

DROP IN

What does success look like for you?

Let me share two examples of success that are meaningful to me. These naturally may be different for you.

Getting Out of Your Own Way and the Power of Confidence

A few summers ago, I was looking for a way to make some extra money. I mentioned in the last chapter that I found work as a tutor, work that helped me build my support network in unexpected ways. But let me share here a bit about how that opportunity came about.

I created flyers offering to tutor students in math and English and distributed them at my local library and sports club. A college student contacted me and wanted help prepping for his business calculus class. I was fifteen years old at the time. I knew that I had the knowledge to teach him college-level calculus, but it was intimidating because I had never tutored before, and I would be teaching someone older than me. I had doubts and was nervous about this job—but I also wanted to make money! I took it, earning valuable experience ... and getting paid thirty dollars an hour!

> **SOMETIMES YOU HAVE TO GET OUT OF YOUR OWN WAY AND PROJECT CONFIDENCE. NOBODY DOUBTED MY ABILITY—EXCEPT ME.**

What's the lesson here? Sometimes you have to get out of your own way and project confidence. Nobody doubted my ability—except me. I asked Jack, the college student, what he thought of a fifteen-year-old tutoring him. His response: "If you know what you're talking about, why would I have a problem?"

Self-Belief and the Numbers Game

That's one success story. My second involves my interest in finding a research internship. I made a goal to conduct research with a professor during the summer. I spent months cold-emailing more than fifty professors. After a few months, I finally heard back from two. One said no. The other said, "Let's talk."

I connected with the second professor, Lea Dunn, a professor at the Michael G. Foster School of Business. I talked to her about my interests and different passion projects I am pursuing this summer—including this book. She told me that she was impressed but would get back to me. I admit that I was disappointed; I thought she was just letting me off easy. But a few weeks after our call, I received an email saying that she had talked to colleagues at Indiana University Bloomington and Nanyang Technological University, and they would all like to start a brand-new research project with me.

This taught me three things:

- If something means enough to you, don't give up on it. Keep selling yourself and trying to land that opportunity because you never know who will resonate with your hunger, drive, and passion and give you a chance.

- It doesn't matter if other people are encouraging. You're done for when you give up on yourself. I almost gave up pursuing research, but I just needed to be patient. A lot of times in life, you go through many more nos to get to a yes. Opportunities are a numbers game.

- I'm awesome. (It's OK to cheer for yourself as loudly as you cheer for other people—it's all about being your own best friend, remember?)

It's clear that success is a numbers game. When I was approaching professors about an internship opportunity, I knew that I needed to email fifty to get one yes. You can't just make one or two attempts and then consider it a failure. The other piece of the "numbers game" is the idea that you miss 100 percent of the shots you don't take. If I hadn't emailed as many people as I could, while still staying productive and efficient, I would have missed the opportunity to get the answer I wanted.

As I think about success, I realize that persistence matters. If you don't stick with something that is meaningful and will get you a return on your investment of time and effort, then you're not going to be able to fully capitalize on that opportunity that you have in front of you. You need to get comfortable selling yourself—this one is still challenging for me—but it's important to be able to present yourself to others and discuss what your goals are and what you've already accomplished. Finally, when you experience setbacks or failure, you need to get over it quickly. I'll talk about this more in the next chapter.

MULL OVER

There are three foundations of success that I would like to discuss in this chapter: maximizing opportunity, becoming your own hype man, and having a steady focus on your goals.

Maximizing Opportunity

There's a quote that my dad often repeats that's attributed to the Roman philosopher Seneca: "Luck is what happens when preparation meets opportunity."

I have my own addition to Seneca's philosophy. I call it "My Golden Rule": Never wait for opportunities to come to you. Go and get them.

"MY GOLDEN RULE": NEVER WAIT FOR OPPORTUNITIES TO COME TO YOU. GO AND GET THEM.

I don't believe in the idea of luck—of random moments of good fortune that happen just because. Luck implies that outcomes can't be influenced by your actions, and in almost every case, that's simply not true.

Here's one more quote to think about. This one's from quarterback Russell Wilson: "The separation is in the preparation." You increase your chances of success if you're prepared to seize opportunities when they come.

Opportunities come to you when you look for them and get creative in positioning yourself to get what you want. Hard work can get you closer to your goals, and it can also increase your chances of coming across opportunities that you might not otherwise have found.

Following My Golden Rule requires you to be proactive and creative. You have to be vigilant—always looking for new challenges and new chances to make progress toward your goals. That's where you'll find success—by capitalizing on opportunities.

Becoming Your Own Hype Man

Hype can imply deception, even lying, but that's not what I mean here. When I talk about hyping myself, I'm referring to the idea of branding and promoting, a kind of marketing strategy.

Yes, selling yourself so that you can seize opportunities requires self-confidence. But if you've been working through the chapters of this book, you know your strengths. You know what you can do well. And you've seen how small steps can lead to growth.

There are a few strategies I use when I'm finding it challenging to advocate for myself. First, I remember where I came from. It's easy to get lost in other people's accomplishments and end up feeling bad. I keep myself grounded by remembering the struggles I've faced and overcome. Those look-backs are great ways to see progress and to recall that I've been successful before, so I can be successful again. If you feel uncomfortable being your own "hype man," try thinking about it like your best friend is hyping you up. What would they say? If you think about it this way, you're not boasting—you're just repeating what your best friend is saying!

Steady Focus and Trusting the Process

At least once a week, I have to remind myself to trust the process. I'm impatient; I want to do things right away. I am extremely results oriented, so I don't want to wait for success. It's hard for me to accept that it will take time to create something great, or to achieve a specific goal.

A friend once shared with me this quote from Ralph Waldo Emerson: "It's not the destination. It's the journey." This idea of enjoying and appreciating the journey of getting to your goal, of being successful, goes hand in hand with trusting in the process. I've also found that, since most of my stress comes from focusing solely on reaching my goals, when I turn my attention toward appreciating the journey, my stress significantly decreases.

***

In this book, I describe myself as a *self-starter*. I use this term because my vision of success—my journey of self-development and discovery and goal setting—was something that I did based on my own initiative. I was encouraged by my parents, and I was fortunate to have a good support network, but I've committed to take charge of my life, to be proactive when opportunities come, and to be ambitious in challenging myself. My drive to better myself and to reach my goals was—and still is—what inspires me to work hard.

I have a strong support network. But my motivation comes from within, from being my own best friend. Success is something I define. I use the resources and opportunities around me to solve problems and push myself.

PSYCH OUT

How you define success today will very likely be different from how you might have defined it two years ago. Just as your goals change and you acquire new skills, the path to success—and what it will look like when you get there—shifts and transforms as you transform yourself.

JUST AS YOUR GOALS CHANGE AND YOU ACQUIRE NEW SKILLS, THE PATH TO SUCCESS—AND WHAT IT WILL LOOK LIKE WHEN YOU GET THERE—SHIFTS AND TRANSFORMS AS YOU TRANSFORM YOURSELF.

But there are some specific strengths and habits that successful people possess—strategies and techniques that you can use to begin to build a practice of working toward your goals. Business expert

Debbie Allen has studied these techniques and written about them in her book *Success is Easy*.

In Allen's view, successful people share seven consistent strengths:[12]

- *Will to succeed and passion to achieve*: These people have a success-driven mindset. They have a deep desire to achieve more than others. They're willing to move outside their comfort zone and to take action to make positive changes. They don't let setbacks become long-term failures; instead, they learn from mistakes and are able to move on to new opportunities. Contrast that with unsuccessful people who give up too soon and let failures defeat them.

- *Self-aware and self-confident*: Successful people trust themselves and their abilities. They recognize their strengths. Even if, at the beginning, they don't have all the answers, knowledge, or skills they'll need, they move forward, believing that they can develop what they don't already possess. They make strong commitments and are confident sharing their opinions and perspective. Unsuccessful people are afraid to speak up; as a result, they often miss opportunities.

- *Achievement oriented and vision focused*: Successful people know their goals. They are clear about what they're working for and are willing to do the work to achieve those goals. They start with small targets and work their way up to bigger accomplishments and challenges. Unsuccessful people lack this kind of focus and the ability to map a path to success with achievable goals.

---

12 Debbie Allen, "The 7 Strengths and Habits that Successful People Possess," *Entrepreneur*, November 6, 2019, https://www.entrepreneur.com/article/340817.

- *Productive*: Successful people use their time wisely. Unsuccessful people waste time and too often are distracted by activities and pursuits that don't support growth.

- *Unique*: Successful people do things that set them apart from others, whether it's their competitors, their peers, or their community. They do more, and do it better, than everyone else, while unsuccessful people fail to excel and focus more on fitting in than standing out.

- *Opportunity finders*: Here it is, My Golden Rule, this time in Debbie Allen's secrets of successful people—they don't wait for opportunities; they see them everywhere and go after them. They are creative and innovative and willing to think differently. People who copy others, who follow the crowd … they are unsuccessful.

- *Love what they do*: Successful people pursue their goals with passion and enthusiasm. They celebrate their achievements and find happiness in each accomplishment.

EVEN ARISTOTLE ATTESTS TO THIS: "WE ARE WHAT WE REPEATEDLY DO. EXCELLENCE, THEN, IS NOT AN ACT, BUT A HABIT."

It makes sense, doesn't it? Success is a habit—or a series of habits—that shapes how you respond to challenges, use your time, and celebrate the skills and talents that are uniquely yours. Even Aristotle attests to this: "We are what we repeatedly do. Excellence, then, is not an act, but a habit."

POWER UP

At the start of this chapter, I asked you to think about what success looks like for you. I think there's value in considering this carefully.

I asked Denise Mitchell about the steps she followed to achieve success. Denise is a sales manager at the insurance company PEMCO, so she knows a lot about leading and motivating teams and helping others to achieve their goals. Her advice? "I wasn't bound by my role and title. I just behaved like I thought a leader would."

Wubet Girma is a leader who has dedicated her career to creating opportunities for underprivileged Ethiopians through programs focused on skill building. Her advice to people pursuing success? "Try and find what you are here for; what your purpose is; what you're all about. I would focus on not comparing yourself to others, but rather having your own conception of who you are, as there is only one you in this world. So, what it is [sic] about you that you can give? What is so unique about you?"[13]

Spend some time thinking about your unique story, your skills and abilities. This is a chance to practice being your own hype person and effectively promoting yourself. Note down some of the specific talents that you have to offer. Don't worry that it seems like bragging. This is a list only for you.

Start from a place of honesty and authenticity. Find something about which you can accurately say, "This one thing is special and unique and true of me." It might be your ability to sing or dance or play an instrument. It might be your kindness and generosity. It might be your imagination and creativity, or your ability to run fast or calculate

---

13   Laura Berger and Glen Tibaldeo, "Are You a Success? Perspectives from Around the World," *Psychology Today*, October 2, 2018, https://www.psychologytoday.com/us/blog/radical-sabbatical/201810/are-you-success-perspectives-around-the-world.

numbers quickly. Find your one true thing and start there.

Next, note down what success looks like for you. Don't be afraid to dream big. What's the opportunity that you would jump at if it came along? Describe, as clearly as you can, this vision of success.

Now, study this opportunity-of-a-lifetime vision. What steps do you need to take to bring you closer to that opportunity? Maybe you need to commit to one hour a day of training or honing your skills. Maybe it's two hours a day. Perhaps you need to work with a coach or take a class or earn a specific degree or move to a new location. Maybe you need to pursue an internship or a job with a particular company.

Analyze those steps and consider what they mean for you, right now, today. What choices should you make to be able to take these steps? What can you do to commit to them?

You will see that big dreams and big opportunities often don't depend on luck or chance. Instead, almost always, there is a series of steps along the way to success—steps that you can achieve and skills you can practice.

I keep a list just like this. I call it my "Go-Getter" list, and on it I track the opportunities I'm pursuing. Since I strive to make the most out of every opportunity, I get anxious about forgetting an opportunity or idea that I have. This simple list allows me to capture all of my thoughts for me to revisit. Under each opportunity, I include a few bullet points; those are the tasks I need to accomplish to complete my goal.

I encourage you to make your own "Go-Getter" list. Use it to outline your priorities, to define success, to focus your life. When you feel like you're distracted or veering off track, when you need direction, examine that list. Remember your goals, and get back on the right path.

If this feels like a stretch, start by drafting a plan. Pick one goal and write it down. I like to use SMART goals. If you're not familiar with this, it's a strategy to help make your goals easier to achieve by defining them in clear ways. Once you're written your goal down, check to make sure that it's ...

S: Specific. What exactly are you trying to accomplish?

M: Measurable. How will you measure your progress?

A: Achievable. Do you have what you need to accomplish this goal? If not, what skills or tools do you need, and how will you get them?

R: Relevant. Does this goal fit in with your bigger goals in life and how you define success?

T: Timing. How long will it take you to achieve this goal? What's your deadline?

> **DON'T WAIT TO BE QUALIFIED ENOUGH, OLD ENOUGH, MOTIVATED ENOUGH. STOP DREAMING ABOUT SUCCESS. GO WORK TOWARD IT AND MAKE IT YOURS.**

Checking your goals against the SMART standard can help you to think about them in very clear ways—and make sure that they are realistic.

I know that it's tempting to just dismiss some dreams as unrealistic, to think that success is something that happens to other people. It's easy to categorize success as something you'll work toward "someday." But I'm encouraging you not to postpone planning for success. You don't have to wait for "someday"—you can get started right now. Don't wait to be qualified enough, old enough, motivated enough. Stop dreaming about success. Go work toward it and make it yours.

Success comes from capitalizing on opportunity. Opportunities are all around you. Go get them.

NOTES

_____

_____

_____

_____

_____

_____

_____

_____

_____

_____

_____

_____

_____

_____

_____

_____

_____

_____

CHAPTER SIX

Get Knocked Down Seven Times, Get Up Eight

I have not failed. I've just found 10,000 ways that won't work.
—THOMAS EDISON

'm not afraid of failure. Why should I be? It's from failure that we learn some of the most valuable life lessons.

Most famous people have experienced failure—usually more than once. Through the experience of failing, they've gained knowledge, understanding, and often new skills.

I've talked before in this book about how my parents have been important sources of support for me, and at least some of the credit for my attitude toward failures and setbacks is due to my dad. Whenever I've felt discouragement, when my energy is low and I need a reminder to keep going, to persevere, my dad uses the same phrase: "Get knocked down seven times, get up eight."

I chose this phrase as the title for this chapter because it's an important reflection of the determination I try to hold on to when inevitable setbacks occur.

Get knocked down seven times. Get up eight.

The phrase is translated from a Japanese proverb: *Nana korobi, ya oki.*

This proverb reflects the acceptance that failure will happen. But the proverb also says that you will get back up again. You will recover. You will try again. The setbacks will happen; what matters is not how many times you experience defeat, but what you learn from it and how many times you get back up and try again. Things will get better if you have the determination and will to make them better.

DROP IN

I used to be a competitive tennis player until I sustained several injuries to my knee and wrists. I quit tennis, not wanting to risk my health for the sport. At this time, I was looking for a new sport, something less intense. So my dad invited me to play golf with him and some of his friends.

I admit it. My first thought was, "Golf is boring, and I don't want to play any sport with a bunch of old, slow men."

I'm not sure why—maybe I didn't have anything better to do that day—but for some reason I finally agreed to join my dad and his friends.

At the beginning, I was not good. The ball flew everywhere, and I was afraid of getting off the driving range and onto the course, because I didn't want to hit anybody with my ball. There was a lot of *nana korobi, ya oki.*

I liked being outside. I appreciated the fact that golf is essentially a one-person sport that you can play with other people, but in the end, it's just you. You're the one hitting the ball. You're the one trying to better your score with each swing of the club and with every hole. You're the only person you need to rely on for success.

I also began to appreciate the opportunity to play alongside people who were so different from me. If I was feeling stressed about school, I could—if I wanted—share a little bit about what I was experiencing. And my dad's friends would tell me about their own experiences in school and also share the encouraging message that life goes on—that the things that are so important when you're in school matter less and less when you spend more time in the "real world." It was refreshing.

Most importantly, though, golf has taught me to get comfortable with being imperfect. In golf, sometimes it feels impossible to get the ball to go straight, exactly in the direction where I want it to go. I remember when I was first practicing and starting out, I would hit shots that I thought were horrible because they weren't going straight. The people I was playing with were always surprised, telling me again and again that what seemed bad to me—because it hadn't landed exactly where I wanted—was actually a really good shot.

With golf, even the smallest changes make a big difference. A slight alteration of your stance or your grip can significantly change the arc of your swing, the power, whether the ball ends up in the trees or the sand … or on the green.

It's rewarding, that element that small changes can make a big difference. But it's also frustrating. You make a tiny little change in your grip or your grip pressure and suddenly, everything is off.

The way other golfers treated their missed shots shocked me.

They simply said, "Golf is hard," and laughed it off. My coaches and friends would tell me, "Golf is a game of who has the better missed shot." Through golf, I learned to move on quickly and learn immensely from mistakes.

I realized that in the pursuit of perfection, I lost sight of reality and only focused on the negatives of my swing. I didn't see what I was doing well and only focused on the end result—the ball not going straight.

Upon this realization, I started finding ways to encourage myself with positivity and acknowledge the good things that I was doing. Doing this in turn made me motivated to practice more, and to try harder. It takes time to reach your goals and patience to trust the process. If you start with building fundamentals and then work up to your other goals, at some point, you will get to where you want to be.

YOU FALL DOWN, YOU GET BACK UP. YOU HAVE TO GET COMFORTABLE WITH NOT GETTING STUCK, WITH SHAKING OFF A BAD DAY AND TRYING AGAIN TOMORROW.

Perfection is always just out of reach, which makes golf a good sport for me. You fall down, you get back up. You have to get comfortable with not getting stuck, with shaking off a bad day and trying again tomorrow.

MULL OVER

When reflecting on failures, I encourage you to be mindful of not thinking of failure as something that has no value. Rather, practice looking for what you gained from that experience.

One of my favorite teachers in high school told me, "You

learn more from failure than from success." Think about that for a moment, considering your own experiences. What are the events that have inspired positive change in your attitude, your approach to life, or the energy you bring to trying new things? I'm willing to bet that your thinking may have been shaped by experiences that didn't work out the way you expected.

The way I approach the idea of failure is understanding that you have not failed until you give up. Failure is something that shows progress and that you are trying new things. If you aren't failing at things from time to time, that means you aren't trying hard enough to grow. If you aren't pushing yourself out of your comfort zone, experiencing things you haven't done before, you aren't pushing yourself to your limits. Failure is a sign of growth, of change, and of progress. Failure is not something to be afraid of, and if you keep running from it, trying to stay safe, you will never grow. This ties back into the notion of being comfortable being uncomfortable. You need to step outside of your shell to succeed, and that may require trying different approaches in order to find the one that works best. As long as you learn from those failures and change your approach to things accordingly, you should invite failure and cherish it, as that is proof that you are growing.

Failure is not only beneficial because it allows growth, but it's also great because it is tailored to you. Setbacks are unique. Though other people may have experienced the same type of setback before, it did not happen in the same way, with the same emotions and responses. Your experience of a setback will be different from mine, even if we are both striving for the same goal. That's why I say that failures and setbacks are gifts. You've brought your unique perspective to them, and you can uniquely shape what you'll learn from them and how they'll equip you to move forward.

I want to share with you one other event that's shaped my view on setbacks.

It was the summer before my freshman year of high school, and I was focused on perfecting my skills so that I could make the high school golf team. One day, I was walking down to golf practice. About halfway there, I reached the corner, stepped into the crosswalk, and the next thing I knew, I was lying in the middle of the road.

Later, a policeman showed me footage from the traffic camera. I could see a car turning into the crosswalk as I walked across the street. I watched it hit me and saw my body fly through the air. The policeman told me that it was one of the only times he's seen someone of my size and frame get hit like that and not suffer serious injury.

I must have been unconscious for several seconds before I realized that I was lying in the middle of the road. My instinct was to get up, to move, because I was in the middle of the street and I was afraid of getting hit again.

I managed to get to the sidewalk and was sitting there, trying to process what had happened. The woman who hit me had slowed down, but when she saw me move, she started to drive away. I was still holding my phone, so I took a picture of her license plate.

She must have seen what I did, because she pulled over then and got out of her car. She kept repeating, "What are you going to do? What are you going to do?"

I decided to call my mom. When she answered the phone, it took me a few seconds to figure out what to say. Finally, I told her, "I just got hit by a car."

There were people who witnessed the accident and had already called 911, so some first responders arrived very quickly and put me on a spinal board. I remember lying on that board while they asked me questions, looking up at the sky and really understanding for the first time that your life can end in an instant.

I was lucky. I had a concussion and some bruises. Immediately after the accident, I struggled to read—I would look at a book and then have no memory of what I had read. I remember how terrifying that was—how could I get through school, how could I achieve any of my goals, if I couldn't concentrate and couldn't read?

Fortunately, those were symptoms of the concussion, and they eventually disappeared. But other symptoms lingered. I had to do physical therapy. I struggled with neck and back pain.

I still battle anxiety related to that accident. I haven't started driving yet; I sometimes feel anxious just sitting in a car. I have moments, when I'm walking on the sidewalk and a car slows down, that my body goes into panic mode. Even in circumstances where it's clear that the car isn't going to hit me, I have to fight that fear and the instinctive panic that takes over.

I've talked in this chapter about the metaphorical idea of falling down and getting back up, but in this case it was a very real, very physical experience from which I had to recover. I had to work through the physical therapy and the challenges of concentrating.

I did it, though. I worked my way back to playing golf again. I committed to making the high school golf team, and I made the varsity team my freshman year. I

CIRCUMSTANCES BEYOND YOUR CONTROL WILL SHAPE YOUR LIFE AND IMPACT YOUR PLANS. YOU CAN CHOOSE TO BE A VICTIM—OR YOU CAN CHOOSE TO BE VICTORIOUS. IT'S UP TO YOU.

continue to work on my game, striving to improve, and am currently looking to break into single-digit handicaps over the next year.

I'm grateful for the fact that I wasn't seriously injured. But more importantly, I'm grateful for the lesson that you can't predict what will happen next or how much time you have to achieve your goals. I've learned to get up and keep going, to not waste time.

There's a lesson for you, too. Setbacks happen. Circumstances beyond your control will shape your life and impact your plans. You can choose to be a victim—or you can choose to be victorious. It's up to you.

PSYCH OUT

There's something much sweeter about the success that follows a few setbacks and/or really hard work. The A that you get on a test seems to hold more value when it comes from a teacher who's never given you a grade higher than a C.

There's science that proves this and that offers important encouragement to anyone struggling to get back up after falling down. In one study of goal persistence, data was collected from the same group of participants at three separate points in time over a period of eighteen years.[14] At each stage, participants were asked to complete a questionnaire that asked them to rate their degree of goal persistence, with statements such as "When I encounter a problem, I don't give up until I solve it." They were also asked to rate their ability to achieve specific goals, and their ability to find something positive, even in setbacks and disappointments.

The results are very interesting. People who refuse to give up on specific goals or challenges and who frame setbacks in a positive

---

14   Quoted in Christopher Bergland, "Perseverance Cultivates Purposefulness and Boosts Resilience," *Psychology Today*, May 4, 2019, https://www.psychologytoday.com/us/blog/the-athletes-way/201905/perseverance-cultivates-purposefulness-and-boosts-resilience.

light—the people who look for silver linings in every cloud—are at a lower risk for panic disorder, clinical depression, and generalized anxiety. The lead scientists in the study noted that part of the explanation for this better mental health is that people who persevere and maintain a positive outlook spend less time worrying about the future or brooding about the past. Their research shows that determination and perseverance—and a firm focus on your goals—help in your ability to become more effective at problem solving as you think about the ways in which your daily actions impact your ability to achieve your dreams.

In a separate study reported in the *Journal of Cognitive Psychology*, researchers considered the impact that perseverance had on success.[15] In a series of experiments, participants were encouraged to reflect on either their past failures or their past successes, and then scientists measured their ability to complete a challenging cognitive task requiring persistence. The result? Participants who reflected on their past failures had far fewer errors in the cognitive task than those who reflected on their past successes.

This study used something called the "Grit Scale" as a way for participants to provide feedback. The Grit Scale is a creation of psychologist Angela Duckworth, who is a professor at the University of Pennsylvania and the founder and CEO of Character Lab, a nonprofit whose mission is to use scientific insights to help children thrive. Her research focuses on the fact that the secret to outstanding achievement is not extraordinary intelligence or exceptional talent, but instead a blend of passion and persistence. Duckworth calls this "grit." She's written a book about it: *Grit: The Power of Passion and Perseverance*.

---

15 Brynne D. Menichi and Lauren L. Richmond, "Reflecting on past failures leads to increased perseverance and sustained attention," *Journal of Cognitive Psychology* 27, no. 2, 180–193 (2015), https://doi.org/10.1080/20445911.2014.995104.

In the book, she says this:[16]

To be gritty is to keep putting one foot in front of the other. To be gritty is to hold fast to an interesting and purposeful goal. To be gritty is to invest, day after week after year, in challenging practice. To be gritty is to fall down seven times, and rise eight.

I hope that you noticed that last sentence. Yes, it's *nana korobi, ya oki.* Success depends not on your ability to avoid failures, but on your determination and willingness to get back up and try again after you fall down.

POWER UP

I'm learning to get more comfortable with imperfection. I still struggle, of course, when things don't work out the way I've planned—when the golf ball goes into the weeds, or when a great internship is awarded to someone else. It's even more frustrating when I recognize that a setback is due to something I did or didn't do—I waited too long, I missed a deadline, I didn't reach out to connect with someone.

I choose not to waste time dwelling on the past. I do think about it—I learn the lessons I need to learn, and then I move on.

If you're there—in the midst of that setback or failure—let me give you a piece of advice. Don't let a setback or failure go to waste. Don't fail to learn from failure. These are valuable experiences that are tailored to your life. When you feel that you have failed at a pursuit or a project, take time to reflect. Write down everything you've learned from that experience of failing. Consider not just the failure itself, but the process that led to it.

---

16 Angela Duckworth, *Grit: The Power of Passion and Perseverance* (New York: Scribner, 2018), p. 275.

Here is what this looks like for me: I created a Google Drive folder titled "Notes from Failure," and within that folder, I have different documents, containing what I have learned from different experiences. The contents of these documents range from failed interviews, to failed math tests, to failing to create a successful after-school club, to failure of a passion project.

There are others who create a "failure résumé," which describes what you failed at and what skills or pieces of knowledge you gained from that failure.

Here are some steps for creating a failure résumé:

1. Document what happened, what the failure was.

2. Why did that failure happen? List the possible reasons (some you will never know for sure).

3. List the things you could have / should have done differently so you would have succeeded. The point of this step is so that you learn to consider different options in the future and avoid making the same mistakes.

How you choose to document your failures may differ from either of these examples, but I strongly encourage you to capture those experiences and that new knowledge in some way. I understand that it can be difficult to look at failures, so as a first step, just make some notes of what happened—what went wrong. Later, when you're ready, add some more details about the actions you took and what you've learned. The value of failure comes from the knowledge you take away. The idea is that this will become a resource that you can use to prepare for new opportunities. At some point, you may find it helpful to categorize these experiences—like the failure résumé—so that you can look back at specific experiments that didn't work out and take that knowledge on to better prepare for a similar opportunity.

Be grateful for the knowledge you've gained. Take your notes, and put them away in a safe place. The next time you are struggling, the next time you need to make an important decision or are starting something new, look at those notes from those failed experiences and reflect on what you've learned since then so you don't make the same mistakes.

Practice perseverance. Be passionate about your goals. Don't let setbacks define you.

And no matter how many times you get knocked down, keep getting back up.

NOTES

_____

_____

_____

_____

_____

_____

_____

_____

_____

_____

_____

_____

_____

_____

_____

_____

_____

CHAPTER SEVEN

Get Over It

People should not be evaluated by what they have. Rather,
they should be given value based on what they do with what
they have, and how they enable themselves to be better.
—NAMI LINDQUIST

Whenever I read something that inspires me or hear a meaningful quote, I write it down. I have scraps of inspiration all over my room. I also keep a quote bank, where I store many of the phrases or messages that are particularly meaningful to me.

I find inspiration in many different people—writers, musicians, inventors, philosophers. I've shared some of this inspiration in the quotes at the start of each chapter of this book.

But you may have noticed that the quote at the beginning of this chapter is by me.

It's great to find inspiration in the ideas of others, but there's something very powerful in being able to inspire yourself. I want to be positive in my thinking, framing my responses to events and challenges in a way that will not simply help me to persevere in that moment, but that will also provide a foundation from which I can better respond to future challenges.

When I have those moments of inspiration, I write them down. I create my own quotes and add them to my quote bank right next to a quote from Eminem or Ralph Waldo Emerson. I look through those quotes often; each one is tied to a specific memory, and when I read them—especially the ones I created myself—I remember exactly what I was thinking and experiencing when I first wrote those words.

My quotes are sources of inspiration and reminders of the direction in which I want to be taking my life. Creating your own quotes is arguably more powerful than finding motivation in other people's quotes. It's customized motivation, instead of one-size-fits-all. It comes from you. You're the only person who knows all of the experiences you've been through, the nuances, the feelings, the actions you took and those you decided not to take. When you look back at the quotes you've created, you can remind yourself, "I knew this to be true when I wrote this quote." You're giving your future self advice. Your own words of wisdom will always be the most impactful and powerful.

DROP IN

In this book, I've shared many of the strategies that I've used to become a successful self-starter. These are principles I've used to help navigate challenges and push past obstacles.

But sometimes, I forget.

I forget that it can be good to stretch myself and feel a little bit uncomfortable in the process. I struggle to reframe a negative experience in a positive light. I'm my own worst enemy instead of my own best friend. I don't want to get back up after being knocked down. I get anxious about missed opportunities and worry that I'm not measuring up to the standards I've set.

I shared some of these fears recently with Patricia Fripp. She's a successful author and speaker who's an expert at coaching people to become confident public speakers and better communicators.

Her response was clear and simple: "Get over it."

It's one of the best pieces of advice anyone has ever given me. It's straight to the point. Accept your failures, and move on.

Getting over it means realizing that it's OK not to be perfect. Getting over it means not wallowing in regrets. You have to recognize that the past can't be changed. At a certain point, there's going to be a very minimal return on investment in terms of thinking back to your past experiences. Early on, there's often value in reflecting, in getting yourself mentally refocused and reoriented, and in learning from the experience.

> **IF YOU JUST KEEP BEATING YOURSELF UP ABOUT THINGS THAT YOU *SHOULD HAVE DONE* DIFFERENTLY, YOU'RE NOT GOING TO BE TAKING THAT SAME TIME AND ENERGY TO ACTUALLY *DO* THINGS DIFFERENTLY.**

But if time goes by and you're still thinking about what you did wrong instead of what you can do next, you're not accomplishing anything. You're not changing anything.

If you just keep beating yourself up about things that you *should have done* differently, you're not going to be taking that same time and energy to actually *do* things differently.

MULL OVER

Sometimes things may not unfold according to your plan. There's only so much that you can control. If you waste too much time trying to rethink steps you've already taken or decisions you've made—or even complaining about events that have taken place—you're not going to be able to seize the new opportunities that are right in front of you.

This is where *get over it* can be helpful. You want to move past the obstacles that are holding you back—to really get over them.

Successful businessman Rick Barnett shared some helpful advice with me: "No matter where you are, as long as you set your goals and start identifying small things that you can do to change, it can catapult you into much bigger things."

In this book, we've talked a lot about steps you can take and techniques you can practice. It's been a lot of action, action, action—about creating tangible, measurable results.

I'm a results-oriented person, so those strategies are very helpful to me and central to my approach to growth and problem solving. I understand the value of taking action, of pushing yourself and not simply being a passive observer of your life. But not everybody has the same personality as me, so you have to figure out what works best for you.

You're going to make mistakes. It's part of your growth process. To grow doesn't necessarily mean that you're always improving. Growth also includes setbacks and failures, and the beauty about both of these things is that they are opportunities to get back up, learn what went wrong, and try again, this time being a little smarter about your next approach.

When I'm reflecting on progress I've made, I remember that growth and success aren't measured just by how many goals I've achieved. There's growth that also comes from the times I say, "Yeah, I failed at this, but I was able to learn something new from it," or "I tried to approach this from a different angle. It didn't work, but at least I tried and now I know what works and what doesn't."

It's helpful to take that time to reflect on things that haven't worked out as you hoped—it gives you a sense of closure and prepares you for what comes next. It also gives you an opportunity to analyze and dissect the experiences and events that haven't unfolded as you wanted so you can learn from them.

But sometimes, when you linger too long in that reflection period, you end up wallowing. You're no longer learning; there's no closure. Instead, you're repeating the same thoughts over and over, without moving on. There's no plan, no purpose, just regret.

I know what wallowing looks like, because I've been guilty of it myself. I've wallowed on things ranging from bad purchases, to staying friends with people who didn't deserve it, to not stopping my bad habit of biting my nails earlier.

I've wallowed on projects that didn't happen and clubs I started that didn't take off. Wallowing happens. But then you need to move on.

Being a self-starter means relying on yourself and building the skills you're going to need—and learning to get over it when things don't work out as you planned.

PSYCH OUT

Your ability to move past adversity and challenges will significantly impact your ability to lead a happy and meaningful life. Psychologists have identified the importance of resilience—the ability to "just get over it"—as a key element of success and personal growth.

Resilience is your ability to adapt to problems and stress. Resilient people don't allow traumas and negative experiences to define them; instead, they reflect, learn, and then *get over them.*

The good news is that resilience isn't a personality trait that you're either born with or doomed never to possess. There are strategies you can use to improve your resilience.

Psychologists recommend focusing on four core components of resilience—connection, wellness, healthy thinking, and meaning.[17] It doesn't come easily; you'll have to practice to learn how to strengthen your capacity for resilience. But that time and focus will pay off. Becoming more resilient will help you learn from difficult and challenging experiences and then move past them.

Let's take a few moments and dive deeper into the American Psychological Association's recommendations for building resilience. First is *building connections.* We've discussed the importance of creating a strong support network, and resilience is one benefit of those strong connections. Remember that these connections don't have to be your peers, other people at school, or your coworkers. They may be older or younger. It may be a group that shares your interests in hiking, photography, or gaming. But take the time to identify those people who care about you, who can help you get over setbacks and will celebrate your successes.

Next is *wellness.* Much of this book has focused on good mental health, but clearly there is a place for being mindful of taking care of your body in any discussion of being a self-starter. Your body needs specific resources to function well and help you succeed, so it's important to recognize those resources and provide them. Sleep, good nutrition, exercise—we all know what's needed, but it's important to

---

17 American Psychological Association, "Building Your Resilience," 2012, https://www.apa.org/topics/resilience.

prioritize them if you're preparing to take on new challenges.

Healthy thinking has been a theme in this book, so I'm glad that the American Psychological Association has included it as one of their key components of resilience. Reframing your expectations, learning from your past, and drawing on reminders that you have faced challenges and overcome them are all powerful tools to support healthy thinking.

The final component of resilience is the idea of finding *purpose or meaning*. The idea of finding your purpose shouldn't be a one-off task; I think it's a lifelong process, in which you set new goals for yourself as you achieve the old ones. But part of the process of finding purpose or meaning in your life is asking, "What's next?" when you encounter a setback or challenge.

Sometimes circumstances are beyond your control. Sometimes there's nothing you can do to fix a specific problem. You can't go back in time to correct a mistake you made or seize an opportunity you overlooked.

Instead, you have to ask, "What's next?"

The events may be beyond your control, but how you respond is within your control. You can choose to wallow, to complain, to get angry.

Or you can ask, "What's next?"

What's next means looking ahead instead of behind. *What's next* means

THE EVENTS MAY BE BEYOND YOUR CONTROL, BUT HOW YOU RESPOND IS WITHIN YOUR CONTROL. YOU CAN CHOOSE TO WALLOW, TO COMPLAIN, TO GET ANGRY. OR YOU CAN ASK, "WHAT'S NEXT?"

identifying a new opportunity or a new goal. *What's next* means recognizing that you can always get back up after being knocked down. As your own best friend, you should love yourself too much to let yourself make the mistake of staying stuck and being regretful. Pick yourself right back up, and chase what's next.

POWER UP

As this book comes to a close, I'd like to ask you: What's next?

Maybe you need to spend time holding your own hand, recognizing what is special and unique about who you are and identifying how those skills and experiences can equip you for success. Maybe you need to learn how to shake loose from the labels other people have put on you and choose new ways to identify who you are. Maybe you've been inspired to pursue a new opportunity; maybe you're learning how to get over setbacks.

I don't like to use the word *journey*—it's overused and is a little bit cheesy—but I don't know how else to describe this process of building skills and celebrating growth and bouncing back from challenges. It's a journey.

And wherever you are on that path, my suggestion is to look ahead, not behind—you're not going backward.

I talked earlier in this chapter about creating my own quotes. I encourage you to try this. Make your own quote bank—a Word document or a piece of paper that holds all of your epiphanies and original quotes. Think about the words of wisdom you would share with your younger self, and write them down. Find inspiration in your own thoughts and ideas.

If you're struggling to create a meaningful quote, try writing a letter to yourself instead. Describe a challenge that you're facing or something you've accomplished recently. Celebrate the small successes as well as the big. Share the insights you've gained, and then place that letter somewhere where you'll be able to find it when you need a reminder of what you can do when you try.

I encourage you to take time for self-reflection, maybe through a journaling exercise. Write down your answers to these questions:

- What have you learned from this book?

- What new discoveries have you made about yourself?

- Which exercises worked for you?

- What new goals, new road maps, new strategies do you want to implement in your life?

In three months, come back and look over your answers to these questions. Do you see progress? What worked, and what didn't work for you? What new things would you like to try? Are there chapters in the book you need to revisit?

My goal when I started writing this book was to be a resource for others—a kind of older sister who could share her experiences and the strategies that had worked for her. I knew that others had faced similar challenges to those I had worked through. There were others who had been bullied, who felt shy, who had big dreams and big ideas but lacked the confidence to act on them. I knew that the knowledge I had gained through hard work and effort had equipped me to take the steps to better myself, and that knowledge would be valuable to others like me. It's funny—writing *Becoming Your Own Best Friend* has allowed me to develop more as well. The process of writing this has taught me a lot about myself and brought to light some things about myself I wouldn't have otherwise realized.

I've encouraged you in this book to hold your own hand, but I want you to know that I'm holding your hand too. I want you to see that change is possible—and you can create your own change. The best part about your problems is that they are *yours*. You have control over them.

As I've reflected on my experiences and thought about the strategies that worked for me, I've realized that change takes time. It doesn't happen overnight.

But it's also not a one-time opportunity. Every day, you have an opportunity to start again, to try something new.

By talking to other people about this book, by discussing my experiences and reaching out to people whose thoughts and perspectives I wanted to share, I've discovered that my view of success was too narrow. Once, I thought that success meant joining the corporate world, working there for a few years, learning new skills, and then starting my own business.

That was my plan. But as I've considered what it means to be a self-starter and spoken with other successful self-starters, I've realized that there's not a single recipe for success. Success is much bigger and broader than that. A successful life means different things to different people: a meaningful career, an opportunity to change the world, a happy family, safety and security.

Your definition of success will be different from mine. That's good news. Because if there's not one path, one set of skills, one background or training, or one school or job, no single obstacle or setback can prevent you from being successful. There's no deadline for success, and no expiration date for accomplishments. You have your own unique story and timeline.

You are the only person who can give yourself everything you want. Don't wait. Do it now. It's the choices we make and the paths we forge that make us who we are.

Make yourself into something beautiful.

NOTES

ADDITIONAL NOTES

_____

_____

_____

_____

_____

_____

_____

_____

_____

_____

_____

_____

_____

_____

_____

_____

_____

_____

_____

_____

_____

_____

_____

_____

_____

_____

_____

_____

_____

_____

_____

_____

_____

_____

_____

_____

_____

_____

_____

CPSIA information can be obtained
at www.ICGtesting.com
Printed in the USA
FSHW020910111020